Mountain Press Publishing Company
Missoula, Montana
1997

Photos courtesy Flansburg family

Cover art copyright 1997 by Dick Gravender

Map by Nico Tripcevich

Library of Congress Cataloging-in-Publication Data

Haaglund, Lois Flansburg, 1929–
Tough, willing, and able : tales of a Montana family / Lois Flansburg Haaglund.
p. cm.
Includes bibliographical references and index.
ISBN 0-87842-370-2 (alk. paper)
1. Haaglund, Lois Flansburg, 1929– —Childhood and youth. 2. Clinton (Mont.)—Social life and customs. 3. Clinton (Mont.)—Biography. I. Title.
F739.C55H33 1997
978.6'825—dc21

97-39299
CIP

PRINTED IN THE UNITED STATES OF AMERICA

Mountain Press Publishing Company
P.O. Box 2399 • Missoula, MT 59806
406-728-1900 • 800-234-5308
web site: www.montana.com/mtnpress

This book is dedicated to the memory of Mom and Dad.

TABLE OF CONTENTS

ACKNOWLEDGMENTS

My sincere thanks to the following people:

Bill Bevis said one day to our Montana Writers class: "Your stories are important," and he first read and critiqued these stories for an independent study.

Professors William Kittredge and William Bevis wrote endorsements that helped open doors to prospective publishers.

My editors, Gwen McKenna and Dan Greer, transformed a raw manuscript into the reality of my first book.

Cal Smith and Pat Smith Kind told me their memories of living at Dixon with Grampa and Gramma. Their contributions were invaluable.

Olive Flansburg Sol told me that Joe Marling, her half-brother, was the first serviceman from Montana to die in World War II.

Mrs. Emma Nefner Batey of Dixon made us laugh the sad day of Ebby's funeral as she told the story of Grampa's cussing.

Harriett Swartz Norris and Shirley Swartz Keickbusch first mentioned Dunnigan's Barn.

Bob Montelius of Clinton filled me in on significant details of "The Search."

Don and Lucille Norton of Clinton, over coffee one day, graciously showed me their abstract on the Old Place that has been their home for over fifty years.

Wendell Brainard, retired newspaperman and historian of Kellogg, Idaho, helped figure out what the big celebration was about when the family stopped by Kellogg on their trek to Montana.

Chuck and Cookie Mead kindly gave permission to use the two "one log with four up" photos that hung in their secondhand shop in Missoula.

For years my daughters, Ruth Caron and Laura Alvarez, told me, "You can do it, Mom."

At a low point in my life, Cordelia Slater encouraged me to keep on writing.

Ruth Hesselgesser Bennett encouraged me and has been in my corner since I was one year old and she was nine, when Mom hired her to keep me from eating rocks.

Early on in the life of this manuscript Lorrie De Yott did some indispensable computer work for me.

Laurel Haaglund Henley, my stepdaughter, bailed me out of computer troubles time and again.

Ken Browning told me things Grampa had related to him about the early days before he married Gramma and about his jobs in Canada. I regret that Ken never got to read the results of his sharings, for he died in June 1997.

Rex Flansburg helped me most of all with his detailed memory of stories and tidbits he'd heard our Dad tell over the fifty-three years they lived together. Like Dad, Rex has a photographic memory and can tell a good story.

ABOUT THE AUTHOR

Lois Flansburg Haaglund, a native of western Montana, lives near Missoula. She graduated from St. Patrick School of Nursing in 1951, and in 1975 earned a certificate as a family health practitioner from Montana State University in Bozeman. She has worked at St. Patrick Hospital in Missoula, Marcus Daly Memorial Hospital in Hamilton, and St. John's Lutheran Hospital in Libby.

Now retired from nursing, Lois attends the University of Montana, working toward degrees in Spanish and English literature with a creative writing emphasis. She is a member of the Women Writers' Guild of Missoula.

Lois enjoys visiting her brother, Rex Flansburg, in Clinton, and her two daughters and three grandchildren in Los Angeles.

Tough, Willing, and Able is her first book.

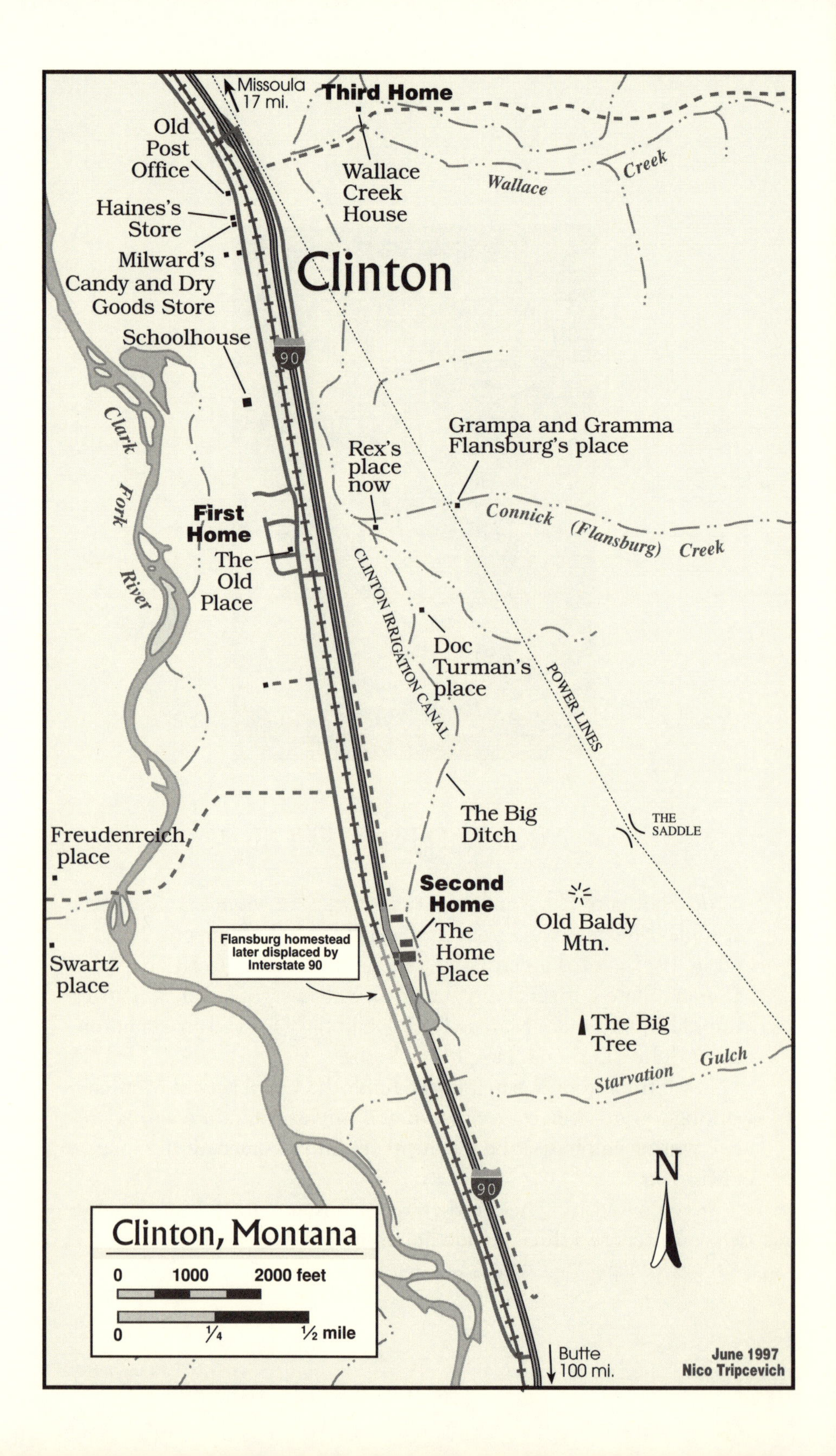
Missoula
17 mi.
Third Home
Old
Post
Office
Wallace
Creek
House
Wallace
Creek
Haines's
Store
Milward's
Candy and Dry
Goods Store
Clinton
Schoolhouse
90
Clark
Fork
River
Grampa and Gramma
Flansburg's place
Rex's
place
now
Connick
(Flansburg)
Creek
First
Home
The
Old
Place
CLINTON IRRIGATION CANAL
Doc
Turman's
place
POWER LINES
The Big
Ditch
THE
SADDLE
Freudenreich
place
Second
Home
The
Home
Place
Old Baldy
Mtn.
Flansburg homestead
later displaced by
Interstate 90
Swartz
place
The Big
Tree
Starvation
Gulch
N
90
Clinton, Montana
0
1000
2000 feet
0
¼
½ mile
Butte
100 mi.
June 1997
Nico Tripcevich

THE ACCIDENT, 1925

IN THE SUMMER OF 1925 Jim Flansburg, the young man who was to become my father, was permanently crippled in the aftermath of a logging accident.

At the top of the hill between Missoula and Arlee on the southern boundary of the Flathead Indian Reservation lies the little hamlet of Evaro, Montana (pronounced "Evro"). That year a sawmill sat at Evaro, and Jim's brother Burl had a contract to fall, deck, and deliver logs to the sawmill. Jim worked for Burl hauling logs from the decks to the mill with a dray pulled by a team of horses. A dray looked like the front end of a low wagon without the back end. The logs were chained to the front, and the log ends dragged along behind on the ground.

My father, Jim Flansburg, as a young man.

Burl's team is pulling five logs on a dray.

Jim gypoed the job, meaning he was paid according to how many thousand feet of logs he could deliver in a day. More speed meant more money.

Jim was good with his canthook, an old-time loggers' tool. A man's canthook was a personal thing like his axe. A lumberjack spent hours honing his axe as sharp as a razor until he had it fixed exactly to suit himself. You didn't mess with a man's axe or you got your ass whipped. A 'jack's canthook was guarded with the same zeal. The handle just fit the owner's hands; it was exactly long enough for his height; and the hook performed exactly as intended every time. With his own canthook Jim could kick loose a log deck, deflect and tilt and turn each log just where he wanted it, and load his dray.

On that summer day Jim pulled up to a new deck of logs, which was enclosed with brush on both ends. He remembered he'd left his good canthook back at the spot where he had just finished hauling out the last deck. An old worn-out hook that belonged to no one in particular lay off to the side.

That's when Jim made his mistake.

Because he was gypoing he didn't want to waste the little time it would take to go back and get his good hook. "This'll do for this one load anyway," he said to himself. He climbed onto the deck and kicked some logs loose. With his good hook he could have caught and guided the logs as they rolled down, but the old one wouldn't hook right and didn't hold.

Wood haulers with their canthooks, Clinton, Montana, early 1920s. Dad is second from left, flanked by the Shapard brothers; Dave Weston is on the right.

Jim ran backward until he ran out of room to go, then fell onto his back on the far side of the dray. About three thousand feet of logs bounced clear over the top of the dray and landed on top of him. The size logs were in those days, three thousand feet probably amounted to two or three big logs plus the "little one" on his chest. He was broken and pinned down and fully conscious. He hollered for help.

The first man there lifted the small log off Jim's chest and yelled, "Git the hell outa there! Git the hell outa there!"

Jim strained and answered, "Hell, man, I can't! I'm pinned in here."

Instead of moving the log over, the man dropped it back down on Jim's chest, and began to run in circles, jabbering, "What'n the hell'r we gonna do?! What'n the hell'r we gonna do?!"

Men ran up from all directions. Burl hooked the team to the logs and dragged them off of Jim. He said that hurt.

Pandemonium set in. Everybody talked at once. An animated discussion of how to get him down off the hill yielded no ideas.

Jim spoke up. "Rig up a stretcher."

Two men set to chopping down a couple of lodgepoles for the handles, and Jim's younger brother, Jake, was sent to the bottom of the hill to get a blanket. Twice he ran all the way down the hill and back up again, asking, "What'n the hell'd I go down there for?"

Jim's oldest brother, Jack, jumped on a horse, galloped to camp, and brought back a sugan, a blanket with a canvas top layer.

No one could come up with how they could hook the sugan to the poles. Jim said, "Use my shoelaces. I won't be needin' 'em for a while."

They stripped the leather shoelaces from his caulked boots, lashed the sugan up, loaded Jim onto it, and packed him down off the hill to the sawmill.

But how to get him to Missoula? The men hit upon laying the stretcher poles across the open wooden bunks of an old Model T log truck and trailer. One end of the poles rested on the bunks of the truck, and the other end on the bunks of the trailer.

They cranked up the old truck. With Jim lying suspended in the hammock of a sugan laced with shoelaces, they chugged down off the twisting, turning Evaro Hill and bounced their slow way over a washboard gravel road to Missoula. By some miracle they reached St. Patrick Hospital, fifteen miles away, with Jim swinging back and forth on his precarious perch.

The worst was yet to come.

Jim's only injury was a fracture of the right upper femur. Dr. G. F. Turman, who was both the family doctor and the physician-surgeon for the Industrial Accident Board, set and cast Jim's leg. The long, unhurried process of bone mending began.

In those days student nurses were akin to slave labor. The girl assigned to Jim that morning probably had more baths to give and units to clean than she could see over. Jim refused a bath, saying he just wanted to be left alone to sleep if he could. She'd probably catch hell from her supervisor if he didn't get that bath. She stated he had to have it.

"Goddam it!" he snapped at her. "Leave me the hell alone!"

She grabbed up a pillow and whacked him across the injured leg. The blow broke the femoral artery, already hanging by a thread from Jim's straining to get out from under the pile of logs. Jim hemorrhaged. Blood poured into his groin, instantly ballooning it up to football size. "Inside of a minute I couldn't say my own name," he said later.

Doctors who happened to be on the ward attempted tourniquets, to no avail. Jim's doctor was in the building making rounds. When he was notified, he ran in, leaped on the bed, and thrust his knee deep into Jim's lower abdomen, shutting off the abdominal aorta. Jim remembered no more. Amid yelled doctor's orders and scrambling and excitement, he was rolled across the hall into the operating room.

Dr. Turman judged Jim to be in such bad shape that an anesthetic could kill him. Jim came to when he felt the searing burn of the foot-long incision. The doctor clamped and tied the severed femoral artery. This saved Jim's life.

Now fully awake and tied to the operating table, Jim called the doctor everything he could lay his tongue to, but the doctor just kept on working, swabbing blood clots out of the wound and sewing it up. Jim could hear the blood-filled sponges splat on the floor as they missed the sponge bucket.

Back in his room Jim received a second transfusion of his father's blood and more saline solutions. Because he was short on both blood volume and sufficient blood pressure to propel around what he did have, his most comfortable position was lying on his right side with his head hanging over the edge of the bed so gravity could help get blood to his brain. Years later whenever he was sick, he lay in that same position for it seemed to comfort him.

Dr. Turman invited several specialists to come in on consultation about the leg. They all recommended amputation. Surgery was scheduled. Members of Jim's family arrived to wait it out. When he was taken to the operating room, Jim told the doctor, "When you git through cuttin', I'm gonna cut it off again right below the ears."

Dr. Turman went to the waiting room to talk to Jim's dad, and he said, "I think I can save it."

"That's what you oughta do then," Jim's dad answered.

Over the next seven months Jim made several more trips to surgery as the doctor fought to save his leg. Because the main blood supply was cut off and collateral circulation took time to form, the toes died and turned black and stinky. They were amputated. Without anesthetic. While the doctor methodically but swiftly snipped off each toe bone back into the live tissue, Jim moaned and cursed.

Years later when Jim told of these experiences, he was proud of his doctor because he knew pain wouldn't kill him, and he couldn't be given a local anesthetic because of the already severely compromised circulation. Jim had high praise for the man who saved both his life and his leg.

One morning when the doctor removed the dressings, he found bedbugs lined up along the wound. Nuns and nurses alike scurried about before the doctor's rage as he called down the hospital's powers-that-be. Large bedsores added to Jim's misery and left scars on the end of his bony spine.

And what became of the student nurse who hit him? Wardmates urged Jim to name her and said they'd back up his story, but he said punishing her wouldn't bring his leg back or make him feel any better. He refused to tell. He never saw her again.

Jim grew thin and gaunt, and his hair turned gray almost overnight. One day in the ten-bed ward the men were guessing ages. Jim was guessed all the way from thirty-five to fifty. He was twenty-one.

His older twin sisters, Olive and Ollie, brought him home-cooked dishes to try to pique his nonexistent appetite. A letter from Olive to their mother dated October 9, 1925, reads:

> *Dear Mama—*
> *. . . He has been eating pretty good since you left and hasn't been in so much pain either I don't think. I just came from the hospital and he is asleep already and its just 8:30 now. . . .*
> *I fixed things for Jim to eat and that way he eats pretty good but if he just gets what they bring on his tray he wouldn't eat hardly anything. So I would like to stay till Sis [Ollie] comes and she can take my place that way. They are going to stay for a while I guess to be near Jim. Then she can cook for Jim and fix him good things to eat. Tonight for supper he ate 2 pieces of liver, some sweet potatoes, 2½ biscuits, 3 cups of cocoa, a glass of milk, and a dish of cranberries. . . .*
> *Love, Olive*
>
> *. . . Sat morn—Mark [Olive's husband] just came back from the hosp and said Jim was resting good. Said the pain was gradually leaving him.*

As the months passed Jim made several more trips to the now-familiar operating room across the hall. Between trips he visited with his wardmates and friends. The day nun in charge of the men's third floor told him he had more company than anyone she had ever seen. Someone brought him a mouth harp. Then he got a button accordion and soon learned to play it; the push-pull sounds worked on the same principle as the mouth harp.

The nun who was night supervisor visited him on sleepless nights. One night their conversation turned to strong people they had known. She told him of the toughest men she had ever seen: One night in 1918 she looked out the hospital's south window onto the livery stable where the Western Montana Clinic now stands. She watched two men sleeping in a wagon box on one of the coldest nights of that winter. All they had over them was a canvas covered blanket. They arose before daybreak and headed east with their teams and wagons.

Jim asked her a few questions about the incident, then said, "That was my brother Burl and me. We'd finished up a loggin' job at Stark up Ninemile, and made it as far as that livery stable that night. We left the next morning before daylight and pulled on home to Clinton."

He told her he and his brothers were used to sleeping out, and had been quite comfortable that night lying on a doodle of loose hay and covered with a sugan.

As a sixteen-year-old in 1918 Jim had written from that job at Stark to his mother in Clinton: "We have a crowd of Sweeds in the bunkhouse that want the windows down so we moved out in the hayshed. . . ."

After seven months in the hospital, Dad stayed with his sister Ollie (behind him). The child facing the camera is Ollie's twin sister Olive's boy, Ode (Olin Smith). The little girl is either Pat or Ebby, one of Olive's second set of twins.

One day a man from the rehab department of the Industrial Accident Board interviewed Jim. Jim told the man he wanted to learn to be a garage mechanic. The man said that since he would never walk again, he would advise him to become a cobbler. Jim scoffed as he told Ollie about it later, "Can you imagine me sittin' on a little stool all day long a-tap, tap, tappin' on shoes?"

About two weeks before he left the hospital, he wrote to Jake:

Missoula Jan 27, 1926

Dear Jake—

. . . I got half the money for my toes $300.00. . . . I have got a bill of sale of all my horses and harness. If you take Dan I might take old Nell, if we can jew him down some and I think we can. I am up on the crutches now and can go like hell. I walked right off the first time I tried it, and I think I will go home Sun. . . . Tell Dad and Ma hell-o for me. and ans. soon.

Jim

PS. Write to Milltown.

In February of 1926, a few days after his twenty-second birthday, Jim was discharged. He left the hospital alone, on crutches. Weak as a sick cat, he navigated his way across Cedar Street (now Broadway), then two blocks east to McCullough Motors opposite the Missoula County Courthouse. With half his "toe money" and $150 of his monthly Industrial Accident money he bought a secondhand Model T Ford touring car. He drove it out to Ollie's in Milltown. For several weeks he stayed with her, eating her good food, and slowly began to regain a bit of strength.

Jim had some very definite plans for the rest of his life.

TOUGH, WILLING, AND ABLE

JIM CAME UP HARD in the 1900s, '10s, and '20s in an industrious family of father, mother, and nine kids. His dad, my Grampa, had the wanderlust to see and work in new country. They traveled and slept in wagon boxes and tents from Missouri to Oklahoma Territory, then to Alberta and British Columbia, Idaho, Washington, Oregon, back to Washington, Idaho, and finally Montana. Dad joined the family in Calgary in 1904.

Life wasn't easy for the large family. Everyone worked long, hard hours. Grampa and the four boys worked their teams of horses in the woods or on dirt-moving jobs. Gramma and the older girls cooked three big meals a day for the family and a crew of hired hands, scrubbed clean the splintery floorboards of cookshacks thrown up at each logging camp, hauled water and cookstove wood, kept eleven persons' meager wardrobes clean and patched, and looked after the younger children. Two of the nine kids became crippled: Zale from polio at two, and Jim from his logging accident at twenty-one.

Theirs was a strongly patriarchal family as was common for that day and age. Grampa literally held the purse strings—he kept the leather money pouch on him at all times carried inside the leg of his pants. Right after their once-a-year payday, the sack he carried home was so heavy with gold coins he had to hold his pants up. By the time he bought Gramma's huge order of food staples, paid off the old grocery bill, the horse-feed bill, and the doctor bill, and bought the yearly pair of shoes for each kid, the sack was pretty light. The rest of the year they lived on credit.

Because they traveled so often from job to job, they had no garden to supplement their diet until they reached Montana. All food was purchased in kegs, barrels, cases, and fifty- and hundred-pound sacks.

Jim was shaped by his upbringing. Grampa was kindly to his wife and family. Jim was, too. Grampa was a hard taskmaster to the boys as they were growing up. So was Jim. Grampa raged and cursed and stomped about when he was overworked or thought someone had shafted him. Jim learned that behavior as well. Both Grampa and Jim were doers, drivers, men who could get the most amount of work done well with the fewest motions.

Unlike his dad, Jim settled in one spot. Except for the last year of his life in a nursing home in Missoula, he lived his adult life at three places all within a two-mile radius of Clinton, Montana.

He had set out to be a logger. When he was reduced to one good leg, he planned to become a garage mechanic. He knew very little about cars—Model T's in those days—but his analytical mind could see how things went together and how they worked.

When he got out of the hospital after that seven-month stay, he stayed several weeks with his sister Ollie. Next he rented a room in Clinton from Ern Terry and got a job with Johnny Baird who owned the garage.

Baird had a bunch of old cars he wanted wrecked out so he could sell the iron. He offered Jim five dollars a car to wreck them out. The tools available in those days for that kind of work were a cold chisel, a hammer, and a wrench or two. Still weak from his hospital stay, Jim set about it. He got so he could wreck out a car a day, big money for those dollar-a-day wage times. Baird said he couldn't stand that much outlay of money so he'd have to cut his wages.

Jim didn't like that turn of events, so he dangled the two thousand dollars the Industrial Accident Board paid him for his leg in front of Baird. Baird took it, and Jim owned a garage. There was also a little grocery store and a tourist court out back with a bathhouse (bright orange with green stenciled letters), campsites, and picnic tables. No motels in those days. The store and shop were at ground level; the living quarters were above.

Not long after he had moved his few belongings to his new home, Jim heard from his sister Olive in Bonners Ferry, Idaho. Her husband drank up his paycheck one too many times. The last time he stumbled in too drunk to stand up, she jerked his belt off and beat him with it. She'd left him and needed a ride back to Montana. Jim drove up and brought her and her four small children back to live with him.

Like his dad, Jim loved kids. Olive's little two-year-old twin girls, Pat and Ebby, would pick up his cute little wrenches and wander off with them. He'd ask, "Whad'ju do with my wrenches?"

They didn't know.

"Go find 'em."

They'd stroll around in the tall grass looking at the tops of the bullpine trees and say, "I don' know."

He told that story years later, chuckling at the memory.

When Olive got a job as head cook at the Northern Pacific Hospital, she took her four kids to live with Gramma and Grampa at Dixon, some fifty miles northwest of Clinton.

George Lehr, Jim's friend since the fifth grade, batched with him off and on. George was raised up Swartz Gulch in what became Matt and Kate Freudenreich's place. He was a renegade. Jim needed a pump belt so he could pump water up from his well, but had no money to buy one. George learned of Jim's need and said, by God, he knew where he could get one. George left late one evening and came back in the middle of the night with a belt. He had gone to some mill where he figured he'd been badly treated once and pulled one off of some piece of machinery. He told Jim he'd slipped in and began to pull it off. It squealed. The sleeping night watchman stirred in his chair. When he settled in snoring again George gave it another pull.

"Here's your belt. I thought I was gonna wake that damn watchman up," he said.

Jim appreciated his friend's interest in his needs, but said, "No more of that." He used the belt though.

When George wasn't batching with Jim, he drove bootleg whiskey from Canada to Butte. In those days of Prohibition rumrunners took the back seats out of their big cars and beefed up the springs so the car wouldn't look overloaded, and they souped up the engines so they could outrun the Federal men. If a rumrunner got caught, the Feds used their own captured cars against them to capture others, so the bootleggers made every effort to locate those captured cars and burn them up.

It was said that all through Prohibition anyone could walk in off the street anywhere in Butte, Montana, and buy a drink. One time the Federal dicks held a meeting in Missoula and were telling all assembled how well they were enforcing the Prohibition laws. Someone asked, "How about Butte?"

"Well . . . I'll tell you . . . ," the speaker says, "Butte . . . is Butte."

George Lehr went by the name of Blair in Butte and eventually legally changed his name to Blair. Jim said if George hadn't married Ann Karsted and straightened up, he might have ended up in prison. Ann had divorced Dr. Karsted of Butte and had five children to whom George became stepfather.

One day Jim met Eunice Mueller, Clinton's new schoolteacher. He began courting her, and they fell in love. This tall, skinny, rawboned man with twinkling eyes and a face split into a wide grin fascinated her. She was charmed by how he could laugh while standing on one leg and two crutches. She saw an indomitable spirit that wouldn't roll over and play dead no matter how adverse the circumstances, and she found this very attractive. She told me years later, "His leg may have been crippled, but his head certainly wasn't."

Their backgrounds were as diverse as they could get. Eunice's people came from solid Missouri farming roots. Her parents met at a business school in Sedalia, Missouri. When they married, her mother became a homemaker, and her father earned their living as a telegrapher, carpenter, and farmer. Because both Grampa Mueller and Eunice's sister, Mildred, had contracted malaria in southeast Missouri, the family moved to Missoula, Montana, for health reasons. Eunice attended the University of Montana for two years, then Normal School at Dillon, and became certified to teach primary grades. She taught at Moiese, Lolo, and then Clinton. Mildred became a teacher, too, and taught until her retirement.

By contrast, Jim had completed the fifth grade and went a little in the sixth, seventh, and eighth grades until he had to go to work on the family logging jobs.

Eunice's parents met Jim when he came to their Howell Street home to court her. They did not approve of her choice, and for several months they took every opportunity to discourage any further interest in "that man." They repeatedly cited all the reasons why she should never even consider him as husband material:

He was crippled; therefore, he would never be able to support her. She would have to support him. In their secret hearts did they think they'd have to support both of them?

He was uneducated. Why, he hadn't even finished grade school.

He didn't go to church.

He swore.

He lived in that shacky-looking place.

He was from a roving logging family "with all those kids."

My mother, Eunice Mueller.

He was not like anyone she had ever known in her life; therefore, a man like that could never make her happy.

He had no refinement.

They flat didn't like him. "Why don't you marry a nice man?" they wanted to know.

What Gramma and Grampa Mueller didn't know was Eunice and Jim were already married. Her parents' constant ragging about him had helped her make up her mind. They were both twenty-four years old when they decided to elope. On July 7th, 1928, they drove to Deer Lodge and were married by a justice of the peace. Jim slipped a reporter five bucks to keep it out of the paper. In Deer Lodge they spotted someone who would know them, so they traveled on to Anaconda to spend their wedding night.

This was the first time that Eunice had ever done anything against her parents' advice, and even though she had made what she felt was the right choice for her, she wept that night for the want of her family's good wishes. The next day she went back to her parents' home, and Jim returned to his garage.

Gramma and Grampa Mueller in their later years.

Within a few days the secret was out, and Eunice moved in with Jim in his little room above the garage.

Eunice had never seen or lived in such a place as her new home over the Clinton Garage and Store. Originally it had been a livery stable. Oil and gasoline fumes wafted up through the cracks in the floor. Wide gaps between the wallboards let in the winter winds. The back wall was not there; instead, a large tarp was tacked over where the back wall would have been if it were there. Jim thought that quite convenient because wood could easily be tossed into the house. It was the best place he had ever lived, and it was all his own. It had a roof and four walls—well, three plus the tarp. For a man who had spent most of his life sleeping in tents and wagon boxes and haymows, this was sheer luxury. It puzzled him to see his new wife's discomfort with the idea of a tarp for a back wall. She mildly protested.

"But look how easy it is to get in the wood," he said. "And there's wood enough ricked up downstairs for a whole year!"

This was a real accomplishment, for he had slowly built up his strength after the long months in bed by chopping and stacking a little jag of wood every day. A big woodpile was a thing he'd vowed to have when he got his own home. While he was growing up, he and his brother Jake had the job of sawing and splitting wood every night for the next day's use. They did this in the dark after they had already put in a full day skidding logs in the woods.

Jim bought groceries the way his parents did. Cases of fruits, vegetables, and canned milk, fifty-pound sacks of spuds, flour, and sugar, and hotcake syrup by the five-gallon bucket occupied every corner of their little one-room home. To get to some place in the room they had to move a sack or a case of food. To find a chair for a guest to sit down they moved a couple of cases. Eunice liked Jim's handy provision and would say, "I'm going to the cellar now," and she'd dive under the bed and come up grinning with a can of peaches.

Eunice's folks understandably wanted the best for their daughter. I wonder if they ever believed that she had the best. Or did they believe that she just put up with what she had?

The Clinton Garage and Store, my parents' first home; that's me at age two in front. At right is the white one-room house that later became our second home. Far right is the old orange bathhouse that became the bunkhouse at our second place.

I know that Mom and Dad respected and adored each other in their fifty-six years together. They honored and were kind to each others' parents. Each was the other's strong arm and advocate and champion, and they shared very definite, well-talked-out common goals. With Jim's health what it was, they both assumed he wouldn't live very long. So their first goal was to gather up a home and a bit of land so that Eunice and their kids need never have to worry about a place to live.

Someone asked them once how they had got along so well for so many years. Dad spoke for both of them and said, "We were always too damn busy to fight."

Certainly they did not always agree; the air crackled occasionally with their animated discussions. Their first real spat came six months or so after Eunice moved in. She was pregnant with me and vexed with morning sickness. This chilly, breezy upstairs place was hardly her idea of a "sweet little nest somewhere in the West," but if she put on enough clothes it was tolerable. The only entrance was by way of the back stairs. That stairway spraddled up like a low-slung ladder and attached itself to the floor of the attic living quarters. The door was the tarp. An outside toilet sat out back and off a ways.

What really set her off was the complete lack of privacy of this one room when Jim's brothers and friends came and parked and stayed for days at a time. They sat in her way as she tried to get meals, told stories and slapped their thighs and laughed till late at night, and made no moves to find a place of their own. They didn't need a place of their own—Jim's place suited them fine. The worst was that Jim thought it was all okay. He was having a good time and couldn't understand why the commotion and lack of privacy bothered her so.

One day she wrote him a note, packed her little black suitcase with the blue lining, and stepped across the road to the Northern Pacific Railroad station where she politely asked the stationmaster to flag down the westbound train for her. In Missoula she hiked over to Howell Street to her folks' house. She offered them no explanation.

Did they think their worst fears were realized? Or their most fervent prayer answered?

That evening Jim drove in to get her.

She asked, "Are they gone?"

"Yes, they're gone."

She climbed into the car and they went home.

Eunice set about learning homemaking skills. Her mother had always said she could do it faster herself than the time it would take to show Eunice how to do it; consequently, she knew nothing of homemaking except how to keep her own room neat. Jim taught her what he knew of cooking, and he eventually learned to avoid telling her how good his sister Ollie could cook. Eunice knew how competent Ollie and Olive were, and she very much admired these new sisters-in-law. She just didn't want to hear it all the time.

A married woman couldn't teach back in those days, and most certainly not a woman "in the family way." In spite of being married and pregnant, Eunice was hired to finish out a school term at Ravenna, a

Dad at his Clinton Garage and Store, now called the Old Place.

little Milwaukee substation about eight miles east of Clinton. Jim ran the garage and store by day and drove a solid-rubber-tired Bulldog Mack gravel truck all night on a local road-construction site. The truck's lights ran on batteries, which he put on the charger as soon as he got home in the morning. When Eunice came home from school in the afternoon, Jim went to bed. She wakened him for supper; he ate, gathered up the batteries, and left to drive the truck all night. He drove half-asleep from berm to berm and woke up each time he hit the opposite berm. Then he opened up the garage in the morning when Eunice went to school. This was how they worked to make ends meet.

I arrived on August 3rd, 1929, at the old Elmore Maternity Hospital at 125 East Fourth Street in Missoula. That square brick building is still there today.

Mom had never been around babies in her life. She did her level best, but it was frightening to be responsible for such a tiny thing that cried so much but couldn't talk. Dad did what he could to figure out my need of the moment, but his own lack of sleep wore on him. As he related it, he'd take all he could of my bawling, then start up the stairs. "Lois'd hear me comin' and go 'WH-A-A-a-a-a . . .' "

I had learned early to fear Dad's anger.

One day Mom saw little red spots all over me. On investigation she found bedbugs in my bed. Horrified, she tore into the house. She yanked back the rear wall tarp and slung out every old sugan that had been lugged in from various logging camps by Dad's brothers and friends. She scrubbed down everything in the room and washed every piece of clothing and bedding in the house. She sprinkled bedbug dust liberally in all the corners, nooks, and niches. She set cans filled with bug powder under each bed leg. Then she designated one day a week as "Bedbug Day." She got rid of 'em.

On October 3rd of 1929 there was the usual traffic on the highway. The next day, October 4th, the stock market crashed. By the 5th no one was traveling—that is, no one but the rumrunners, for they were the only ones with any money.

George Lehr influenced his other rumrunner friends to stop and fuel up at the Clinton Garage. No matter how much gas they put in their big Packards or Studebakers or Pierce-Arrows, they handed Dad a

Mom and me at the Old Place.

twenty-dollar bill and drove off without waiting for change. In late 1929 that amounted to a very big tip. Dad said later, "The rumrunners' trade was all that kept us from starvin' t'death."

In 1931 I was two years old.

Dad's every step still gave him pain.

The Great Depression was tightening down the screws.

Then the highway moved, and Mom and Dad's struggling little Clinton Garage and Store was left high and dry.

THE MOVE, 1931

A SIGN AT DAD AND MOM'S little grocery store and garage at the east end of Clinton, Montana, read: "We don't know where Mom is, but we've got pop on ice."

Dad and Mom had nearly a year of relative prosperity until the stock market crash of 1929, resulting in no traffic on the Old Mullan Road, which meant no business. In 1931 the main highway moved over across the railroad tracks.

In the very midst of the economic depression with several hundred uncollectable grocery dollars on the books, Mom and Dad made the decision to go out of the grocery and tourist court business and move their garage business to the new highway. They bought nine acres two miles east of Clinton from the Clinton Irrigation Ditch Company on jawbone—that is, Dad talked the Ditch Commissioners into selling it to them for nothing down and pay-as-they-could. This was where my brother Rex and I grew up.

Dad and Mom had high hopes for a better life on those nine bare acres. For their "new" house they moved a tiny two-room cabin from their tourist court. Dad put wagon axles under one end of it, let the other end drag, and pulled it to the new place with his homemade wrecker. He tore out the partition making it one room, and this became our front room and their bedroom. A small add-on provided a kitchen and another bedroom.

Next Dad skidded the bathhouse from the tourist court to the new place on log skids pulled by a team of horses. That ugly little orange nine-by-twelve-foot shack served as a guesthouse and later as the hired man's bunkhouse.

They dug a well and set a long-handled pump over it with a tin can full of water nearby to prime it when needed. Way out back they dug a hole and built an outside toilet over it. With that done they again had a home.

Dad's friends helped him put up a good-size log building for his shop and garage. Fifty yards to the east of the shop Hart Refineries erected two five-hundred-gallon gasoline storage tanks. In front of the shop they set up two red, glass-topped gas pumps, one for regular and one for ethyl. You filled the glass top with gas by pumping a lever back and forth; then you released the nozzle in the customer's gas tank, and the gas was delivered by gravity flow. Dad and Mom were in business again.

Dad built pole corrals and a low-ceilinged log barn that held four horses and two cows. Next came a root cellar, an icehouse, and eventually two haysheds and a woodshed. Cow and horse pastures completed their homestead. Whatever money came their way went for things like garden seeds and nails and spikes and land payments. Taxes had to wait until there was enough money to pay them; once it took the entire seven-year grace period.

To Dad this new home was even more luxurious than the one they'd left. To Mom it was a giant step up from their former quarters, for she now enjoyed four actual walls instead of three walls and a tarp, and there were no wide cracks between the walls and the floorboards. Chub Swartz wintered in their Old Place after they moved, and as tough as he was he couldn't stand the keen wind whistling through the wide cracks

Mom and Dad's second place, two miles east of Clinton, where Rex and I grew up.

of the little upstairs room. He thawed out some dirt and mudded up those cracks.

Dad said years later, "If there was a nickel out there, you did whatever you could to make that nickel." He worked in his shop repairing anything, took wrecker calls day and night, took on hauling jobs of all kinds, and got a contract for the grade-school bus run from Nimrod to Clinton. I remember the yowling whine of the drag saw when Dad sawed cordwood to sell. Both Mom and Dad tended the gas pumps and made parts runs to the Motor Supply in Missoula.

Mom made our three-room house a real home. She raised a huge garden and preserved the harvest, and when she got all we needed for the next year she invited neighbor women to come get whatever they wanted of it. Olive Dawley, who bought their Old Place in Clinton, said to me many years later, "At one time I had over a thousand quarts of garden stuff in my cellar that came from your mother's garden."

Mom kept the family's clothes clean and ironed using the going equipment in those days: galvanized washtubs, a washboard, a boiler for the whites, and sadirons heated on the wood cookstove. We didn't change clothes every day like we do now. She did mounds of patching, mending, and sewing with a brand-new Singer treadle sewing machine. This was their first and last purchase on the payment plan, three dollars a month. Those three dollars came so hard they vowed, "Never again!" Though they went in debt for necessities or to buy more land as it came up, they never bought another thing on "the easy squeezy payment plan."

Mom also watched over me, their tiny, first-born, wiggly girl-child. To hear Mom tell it, this was a full-time job in itself, for I "darted here and there like a bird." She once looked up just in time to see her little three-year-old girl running down the white line of the highway with one arm draped companionably around her big dog's neck. And one afternoon when Chub and Catherine Swartz came back out of their cabin to continue work on their well pump, they saw that three-year-old Lois had run the quarter mile up to visit them. I was standing on the edge of the well peering down into that big black hole that had never been there before.

Mom asked Mrs. Hesselgesser if her nine-year-old daughter Ruth could live at our house a few days at a time to watch me so Mom could get something done. Ruth stayed with us off and on for several years and became my chief playmate and companion. Between the main highway and two railroad tracks on one side and a pond and the Big Ditch on the other, my parents and Ruth somehow raised me to maturity.

When Rex came along six years later, Dad built a hog-tight fence to keep him in; but he was as placid as I was hyperactive, and he even shut the gate on himself when he found it open. Mom was glad. His temperament made her life much easier.

Mom and Dad's chief tools of survival during those hard times were grit and gumption, intelligence and know-how. Dad had lived lean all his life, so making something out of materials at hand or getting a job where there was no job was like a second skin to him. Although Mom had been raised on small Missouri farms and had led a more sheltered life than Dad, she knew the value of being able to raise one's own food, and she had the ability to do it.

Their nine acres was an ideal place to weather the Great Depression.

Yet others weren't as fortunate. In those hard days of the '30s the boxcars were full of tramps: good men, family men on the road looking for any work anywhere, drifters who would be drifters even in good

Little Rex and me in front of the old log garage.

times, and bad eggs. A person had no way of telling which kind of hobo it was standing at the back door.

Directly in front of our place was a railroad siding where freight trains pulled over to wait for fast passenger trains to thunder by. Those delays gave hobos enough time to slip off and walk over to our house for a handout. Mom gave huge sandwiches stuffed with venison roast or steak to every bum who came to our door. As she piled two slices of thickly buttered bread to overflowing with deer meat, she'd say to me, "These men are hungry. We must never turn anyone away who is hungry."

For one tramp Mom had nothing handy to fix the usual bulging sandwich, so she filled her big blue mixing bowl with just-picked strawberries, added some sugar, and poured Creamy the cow's thick cream over it all. She gave it to the wanderer at the back door saying this was all she had today. The man's eyes twinkled; he grinned and slowly shook his head from side to side in wonderment, saying, "Strawberries and cream for a tramp. . . . Never heard of such a thing. . . . Strawberries and cream for a tramp."

Tramps never came into the house, but after thanking Mom they either took their sandwich back to the siding or sat on the back steps and ate. Some men offered to chop wood for our cookstove, but Mom said it wasn't necessary. I think she didn't want them hanging around all that long, for who could tell the bad eggs just by looking?

I remember one fellow who insisted she let him pay for his meal in some way. He chopped a nice little pile of cookstove wood; then he took off his hat, held it with both hands over his chest, bobbed a jerky little bow, "Thank you kindly, ma'am," and headed back to the tracks.

Years later I learned that if a place was one where a 'bo could get a good handout, drifters somehow marked it for those following. I believe our house must have had such a mark.

Mom and Dad never turned anyone away hungry—except once.

I was seven. A knock came at the front door. Thinking one of the little Dawley girls had come to visit me, I threw the door open. There beyond the screen door stood a tramp. I was surprised because tramps always knocked at the back door. He was a tin-can tramp, one who carried a gunnysack full of who-knows-what he had picked up along his way, even tin cans to cook with in the jungles if there was anything to cook. He stood there stooped, thin, and pinched, and looked like Walter Brennan with his teeth out except for two yellow snaggles in the front that didn't match. He leaned in close to the screen door. His bright eyes darted this way and that into the house. In a low conspiratorial voice he asked, "Is they eny men folks 'round?"

I knew that Dad was out on a wrecker call, and Harold, the hired man, was way out back irrigating in the three-cornered pasture. Naive and guileless, I answered truthfully, "No." He opened the screen door and pushed the half-opened door aside. His body stink assaulted my nose as he barged past me and sat himself down in Dad's favorite chair. I froze, gaped at him, and felt fear prickles spread over my skin.

Mom came in from the kitchen staring in shock and surprise at the audacity of him sitting there quite comfortably in Dad's chair, legs crossed, his top foot jiggling up and down, perfectly at home. He instructed Mom, "Now don't go to any bother about me. I eat anything." And he settled back waiting for supper.

Mom's jaw dropped, closed again, and without a word she motioned for me to come into the kitchen. We watched out the kitchen window for Dad to come back, and watched the tramp in case he picked up anything for his sack.

After what seemed an awfully long half hour or so, we heard Dad's wrecker pull in. Such relief! I thought, "Everything's gonna be all right now."

Mom went out the back door and I saw her speak to Dad. Here came Dad limping fast on his bum leg. He burst into the front room with, "What'n the hell'r you doin' here?!"

The tramp started to answer, but Dad shouted him down with, "Get your goddamn hell outa here!"

Mr. Tramp grabbed his bundle and scurried out and away as Dad cussed him out the door and off the porch. Down the road he jogged, really picking 'em up and laying 'em down, his tin cans a-rattling.

THE FIRE, 1937

I WAS SEVEN YEARS OLD when Dad's shop burned down. Those days there was no fire department, and the only phone was at Haines's Store two miles away.

Late on a Saturday afternoon in January a highway patrolman stopped and asked Dad to take a wrecker call somewhere east of us. Dad checked the shop stove. It was completely out. He left in his wrecker he had built from a 1930 ton-and-a-half Chevy truck, painted bright orange with "CLINTON GARAGE" stenciled in black on both doors.

At four that afternoon I mentioned to Mom about "those funny-looking puffs of smoke" poofing from the chimney every few minutes. Since we did not have electricity until later that year, she took a flashlight out to the garage and checked things over. The stove fire was still dead out.

She had no more than returned to the house when "WHOOF!" the whole roof rose up, shuddered, and fell back onto its log walls. Immediately black smoke boiled and rolled out, blotting out all daylight as a keen east wind carried it down upon us.

Mom thrust the flashlight at me, saying, "Run to Dyermans' and ask them to go for help!" The Dyermans lived a quarter mile away.

No more than a dozen steps from the house I became engulfed in blinding blackness and got lost. The flashlight showed nothing but heavy smoke, and I couldn't see my own hand in front of my face. I panicked and screamed, "Mama! Mama!" Following the sound of my frantic cries she located me; then, still holding onto the clothesline with one hand, she groped our way back to the house. My lungs burned from the acrid rubber smell, and not until we reentered the house could I get a deep breath.

Had I been able to reach the neighbors there was nothing anyone could have done, for within three or four minutes from the time it blew, flames were reaching for the sky.

Mom gave me strict orders to stay in the house and keep little Rex with me. He was a year and a half old and watched the flames with wonder.

Mom ran out and moved our gray '34 Ford car around back by the icehouse; then she tried to move a ton-and-a-half truck that was also parked alongside the garage. She got it started but it died. Men had arrived quickly from out of nowhere, and they bodily picked the truck up and packed it out of the way. It had got so hot that the windows had melted down into the door.

There was no way to save anything else. Everything went. Barrels of oil, racks of tires, all Dad's tools, three of his cars, and enough dry lumber stored upstairs to build on a bedroom for each of us kids. Dad had just finished servicing his school bus, and it was sitting in the garage to be sure it would start on a cold Monday morning. Had it not been out on the run, the wrecker would have gone up, too, for it was always kept in the garage to be instantly ready for a call.

There was no insurance on any of it. Who could afford insurance when it took everything just to keep working and eat?

When men began to pour in to help, Mom came back into the house. With her there I felt safe again and could relax and watch the drama unfold before me. The hoses on the gas pumps burned off. Flaming gas ran down the highway. I was fascinated by the scene of a Greyhound bus stopped, and cars lined up behind it, and faces at the windows held by the sight of the spectacular fire.

Flying sparks set afire two bullpine trees in our side yard, and George Dawley came in to evacuate us. Mom wrapped little Rex up in a blanket, head and all, and handed him over to George who asked, "Which end's up?" We all laughed and welcomed the break in the tension. He led us out by the garden, safely back from the rear of the garage, and settled us in our warm blankets in the back seat of an old green 1924 Dodge car where we watched the fire burn. Now it was dark. Our faces lit up with the reddish glow.

A line of brave men stood holding up the back wall of the burning garage. Each man stood holding a two-by-six up against the top of the back wall so that when it fell, it would fall forward into the fire rather than backwards on the white-and-green WPA-built toilets, then to the trees, the hayshed, and up the mountain behind our house. The toilets were close enough to the heat that they remained blistered the rest of their lives.

And then I saw the scene that transported me from awe and adventure to tears. There behind the line of men holding up the back wall stood Dad, his hands in his back pockets, palms outward. Just standing. Watching. He who could always do something constructive in any situation could do nothing but watch his and Mom's livelihood burn to the ground. Though I was only seven I was well aware that they had worked long hours for nine years and had thus far prevailed against the Great Depression itself with Dad on one good leg and Mom carrying her heavy load right along with him.

The morning after the fire I got up before anyone else and went out to see what was left. There lay a long rectangle of ashes with tiny tendrils of wispy smoke rising from it here and there. Twisted metal of car and truck bodies stuck up above the ashes in mute agony. At the edge of the ashes near the back where the tool bench had been lay a dull thing that had once been a shiny six-inch crescent wrench. I thought of how Dad would say to me, "Hand me a six-inch crescent wrench, honey."

"This one?"

"Yep. That's my good girl."

That burned wrench symbolized great loss to me, for I imagined that with no garage and no tools how could I ever again bring Dad his wrenches and enjoy his comradeship and approval that I so desired.

As we kids slept and kindly neighbors watched the remnants of the fire, the folks talked all that night. They figured out how it must have started even though the stove was cold dead out. The log walls had settled, but the brick chimney didn't, and a spark from the morning's fire must have begun to smolder in the tarpaper layer between the ceiling and the tin roof. When it reached air, it blew up.

Dad and Mom decided to rebuild and planned to collect whatever they could of the $3,000 owed them on various garage accounts. In the morning Dad got into our '34 Ford to begin his rounds of collecting. The car wouldn't start. He scraped around in the still-warm ashes, found what tools he needed, and got it started. He drove all day and came home that evening having collected $3.

Dad had a contract for hauling schoolchildren from Nimrod to the Clinton school and from three miles west of Clinton to the school. It paid $160 a month, but now they had no bus and not five cents to their name.

To get another school bus H. O. Bell sold him a truck for nothing down. Dad made the trip to Detroit to get it, then drove it to Lima, Ohio, to get the bus body put on, then home. Until he got back with the new bus, Mom fashioned "SCHOOL BUS" signs for the fronts and rears of ours and several neighbors' cars, and the school kids never missed a day of school. Dad made the deal with H. O. Bell to take only his expenses out of the $160 and give Bell the rest.

Hart Refineries manager, Mr. Gregg, told Dad of a meeting he had attended between Charlie Hart and his partner, a Mr. Green. Green wanted Dad to pay for the thousand gallons of gas that ran down the highway after the hoses on the gravity flow pumps burned off. Hart's answer was, "This man's lost enough. We can stand that loss." And that's how it stood. Hart Refineries continued to sell Dad gas and oil, and they carried him on the books while he paid as he could.

Motor Supply did the same. Ted Jacobs at the First National Bank backed my folks all the way. Dr. George F. Turman took care of our medical needs and was a good friend as well while the folks got back on their feet.

The Missoula Mercantile Company (now The Bon building) sold everything in those days from groceries to hardware to implements and clothing, even licorice ice cream cones. We called it the M.M. Mr. C. H. McLeod, the head man of the M.M., gave Dad and Mom credit for anything they needed, and they paid as they were able.

C. H. McLeod was an unusual man. The story goes that he once approached a man picketing the M.M. Company in the rain. McLeod asked the man, "Don't you have a coat?"

"No," answered the picketer.

McLeod said, "Well, you go in and get a coat and charge it and tell 'em I said so." And McLeod packed the man's picket sign for him until he got back.

These and others were the sort of business people who helped Mom and Dad after the fire in 1937. All were eventually repaid in full. By early spring a bigger stucco garage had been raised on the site of the old log one.

On a warm June day I climbed up the face of Old Baldy Mountain that rose abruptly behind our place to the Big Tree, my favorite get-away spot. Sitting up there on the Big Tree's gnarled roots (themselves as large as small trees) I could, like God, survey all my queendom and all things precious to me.

I saw the Clark Fork River winding its way along the valley floor at the feet of the far mountains. One mountain bore the familiar imprint of an old fireline like a wishbone with its little end up. I fancied the clump of trees on the skyline of the farthest hills to be a castle.

I looked across my valley to Swartz Gulch a mile away and pictured Chub Swartz when he saw the flames and jumped aboard his saddlehorse and pounded over to rescue us from a fire—where? The house? Would he get there in time to save us? What would he find? He rode his horse so fast and hard that evening that he was the first person to arrive, but it broke his saddlehorse's wind and the animal was never any good after that. As I sat gazing over at the Swartz and Freudenreich places, I thought of the fun Mom and Dad and Chub and Catherine had over a pinochle game at our house the night before.

On my right lay the hamlet of Clinton with its tiny houses and the square box of the schoolhouse of white clapboard with green trim. I could see the Old Place where Dad's original Clinton Garage sat before

The old Clinton schoolhouse.

The new garage. Dad sold Hart Refineries gas and Gates tires; the Gates man gave me a small rubber ball that bounced beautifully off the garage wall.

the highway moved and they moved here with it. My friends, the little Dawley girls, lived there now. The NP Railroad tracks ran through the narrow valley with the Old Mullan Road and Highway 10 on either side of it.

Directly below my perch lay our buildings. There was the new stucco garage. I had watched Johnny Baird build it out of Lew Miller's lumber. When the weather warmed so that it didn't freeze, Lee Wells and Johnny Aktepy stuccoed the outside. That wall was a great place to bounce my little Gates Rubber Company ball. Dad remarked once that it could crack the masonry, but he said he didn't object to me doing it. I got to be a pretty good catcher.

Out front I could see the two new red-and-white gas pumps. I watched as Mom waited on a customer, then went back into the house to make change. I saw her count it into the customer's hand as she had taught me to do.

It was washday, and the clotheslines were full of whites and darks waving in the gentle breeze. Rex, now two, pulled his little red wagon out by the root cellar on some important errand of his own making. Mom's big garden was up, and we were eating strawberries and cream again.

Out in the three-cornered pasture lay Creamy, our Jersey cow, chewing her cud. Dad's black saddlehorse grazed alongside the workhorses. There was Fan, the sorrel mare with her light mane and tail. And Big Kneed Nell, the bay mare.

That morning I had handed tools to Dad as he lay under a car on his homemade scooter. I had saved him time and painful steps. He grinned and said, "I wouldn't take four dollars for you, right now."

From my solitude I sat surveying my landscape, my people, my home. Life was good in my world.

I MAKE THE ROUNDS, 1938

I WAS NEVER BORED. My company was Rex, my little brother six years younger, and occasional visits with the little Dawley girls, Fern, Rosie, and Tee Wee (Violet), whose folks had bought Dad's Old Place in Clinton.

For the most part I was a solitary child; yet I was never lonely, for there were so many fun things to do around our place. If no errands needed running, or the garden didn't need planting or weeding or picking, or if the woodbox had enough cookstove wood in it to last the afternoon, there were oodles of things to do by myself, like cutting out paper dolls or movie stars' pictures or playing solitare.

Or I make the rounds. I amble out past the back of the shop. Its big sliding back door is open, and Dad is in his mechanic's skullcap working on some piece of machinery with greasy black hands. He sees me and sings out, "How's my good girl?" and I grin, give a little dancey step, and answer, "Fine!"

I go by the bus garage, which had once been the old Ravenna schoolhouse where Mom taught a few months, back when I was "on the way," as Mom called it. There is a blackboard in it yet, and some chalk and an eraser, but I don't stop. Today I am headed for some real excitement.

I stand a moment in the door of the empty little log barn to let my eyes get used to the dark, and I savor the earthy smells of horse manure and harness and hay. Then, ever so quietly, I tiptoe to the oats bin back of the cow stalls and—quick!—I throw open the lid and watch the mice skitter for cover. They live happily and in plenty out here, and undisturbed until either I or the cat comes around.

I climb over the corral poles (gates are for old folks) and make my way to the headgate that lets in our irrigation water from the Big Ditch. Here yellow-and-black water snakes sun themselves in the mists along the water-soaked boards. Even though I am on the lookout for them, I yip and jump straight up when one slices across my path. I throw big rocks and kill as many as I can, watching in morbid fascination as they writhe and die and turn their gray bellies to the sun.

Ice chips would taste good. I wander back from the ditch bank to the icehouse. I crawl up into the cool darkness and, like a dog digs with his front paws, I dig down into the old, dark red sawdust to a block of ice. With an old table knife I keep there for this purpose, I chip away and get several slivers. I wipe off the sawdust on the front of my bib overalls, and suck on ice chips as I sit and dream and relish the cool comfort of my spot while outside it is hot.

Our icehouse is made of untreated railroad ties spiked together, one on top of another. Last winter I watched Dad and Chub Swartz take turns sawing blocks of ice with a single-handed crosscut saw on the Big Ditch Pond below our house. As the blocks came loose, the men snagged them with the ice tongs and loaded them onto a sleigh. Fan and Big Kneed Nell pulled the sleigh over to the icehouse. There the men packed all sides of each block with ancient red sawdust so they wouldn't stick together when they were taken out to either cool our icebox or to make a batch of ice cream.

Mom says we're going to have ice cream after supper. As I sit sucking on my lovely piece of ice, Dad comes in to get a block. Together we dig down around one until Dad can get the ice tongs on it. It comes out easily. He carries it in the tongs over to the side yard to the pump and pumps a bit of water over it to get the sawdust off. With an old axe he chops the block in two and puts half of it in Mom's icebox on the back porch. The other half he chops into smaller chunks, puts them in a gunnysack, and crushes the ice with the flat of his axe.

Mom comes out the back door carrying the canful of ice cream makings she has put together—cream, eggs, sugar, junket, vanilla, and a dash of salt. Making sure the can lid is on tight so that salt won't get in and spoil the whole batch, she fits the can of makings into the bottom of the wooden ice cream freezer bucket and fastens the crank on top. Dad begins to fill the bucket, alternating a layer of ice and a layer of rock salt clear to the top. Then he begins to turn it.

"Can I do it?" I beg.

"Have at 'er!" he says, knowing that as soon as it begins to harden I will just as eagerly want to give the job back to him. I watch the cold, salty water drizzle out of the hole in the bucket's bottom as I crank. Dad adds more ice and salt as it melts. Whenever Dad is too busy to do the ice-and-cranking job, he has the hired man do it. Mom packs it and cranks it herself sometimes, but Dad or a hired man always gets the ice out for her.

Little three-year-old Rex has just joined us from his important business in the sandpile. As he grows older he will transfer his construction and logging business to "the mountain" (the top of the root cellar), but this afternoon he trundles his little red wagon over to the ice cream site.

Rex and I sit and watch the turning and wait for the dasher to come out. "Don't scrape off too much!" we say, and with spoons we slick the dasher clean. So good! Mom replaces the can lid, repacks the bucket with more ice, tucks the gunnysack over the top, and our ice cream awaits dessert time.

Dad takes a rare rest. He sits with his back against the pump and has himself a smoke of a Velvet roll-your-own while he waits the few minutes till supper.

A typical picture of Dad. As he sits on the top rail of the corral waiting for the horse trough to fill with water, he rolls a "pill" (a cigarette). This is a good view of his old shoe.

"Supper's on!"

Mom has fixed venison steak, mashed spuds, milk gravy, green beans with bacon and onion bits, and pickled beets. Dessert is ice cream served in mush bowls with crushed strawberries on top—as much as you want. Whoever happens to be here at suppertime joins us, and Dad sings out, "Well, tie into 'er!" All the vegetables came from our garden. Creamy provided the milk for the gravy, us kids' milk to drink, and the adults' coffee cream. The bacon was once one of the pigs in the pen out by the barn. The venison steak grew up as a deer in the hills behind our place and grazed in our pasture on moonlit nights.

In those days of the '30s everyone ate venison. Nelle Hughes said that the women who brought sandwiches to the doings at the Clinton Club House would say to each other as they sampled their neighbor's sandwich, "My, this is good. What is it?" "Ham" or "chicken" or "beef" would be the answer. They were all venison, and everyone knew it. Later on in the '40s the classic government official was a forest ranger who came to count the two cows you were turning out on the hills, but in the '30s the egghead government man was always the game warden. Hunting out of season was no sin then, for survival is not always strictly legal.

Trusted friends share our venison supper tonight, so Dad tells the one about Chub Swartz and the game warden:

"The word's out that the game warden's nosin' around Clinton. When Chub got the tip, he an' Catherine were right in the middle-a cannin' their deer up in a boiler. So while Catherine an' Eunice were out tearin' down the woodpile and pokin' jars in and coverin' 'em up with cordwood, Chub grabs the hot boiler offa the stove, jars'n all. He shoves it in his rumble seat and starts runnin' up'n down the road with it. He glances back and there's *steam* a-rollin' up outa the back of his car!"

Everybody roars.

"He pushes the boiler into a culvert and drives off. Comin' back down the road he sees steam pourin' outa both sides-a the culvert! So he jammed it all back into his rumble seat an' just kept runnin' up'n down the highway till it cooled off an' the coast was clear."

Dad shakes up and down with laughter at the ridiculous picture. Then he says, "Turns out the game warden was after somebody else!" And everybody laughs some more.

Conversation flows nice and easy, and similar stories are told this typical summer evening. Life is good. I am nine.

THANKSGIVING AT DIXON, 1934

MY NAME IS LOIS. I'm five years old. We are going to Dixon today because it's Thanksgiving. That's where my Daddy's momma and daddy live. I have a dress on today because it's Thanksgiving and we're gonna eat one of Gramma's turkeys. It's a long, long ways to Gramma and Grampa Flansburg's—all the way from Clinton to Dixon. . . .

We're in Dixon now. . . .

There was a big, long, snow-covered hill right behind the schoolhouse. Dad took a run at it, but we co-o-ouldn't quite make it, and we backed way down to the bottom again. On the next try I announced I would help.

"I'm sitting heavy, Daddy!"

As we slipped and slid and scratched and the car whined to make it the last little pitch, I scrunched down real hard in the back seat and rocked back and forth, then bounced up and down to help.

"We made it! Here's Gramma and Grampa's house at the top of the hill!"

Mom and Dad grinned at each other in the front seat.

Grampa picked me up and gave me a kiss on the cheek, which I promptly wiped off. His big gray mustache was wet. He chuckled and set me down.

His mustache was long and untidy. Once, while watching him eat a dish of canned tomatoes, I sat open-mouthed in rapt attention, focused on those many long hairs that seemed to be getting mixed up with the tomatoes. He held his dish up on his chest and spooned them in; some juice hung up on the mustache. Then with two deft swipes with the top of his forefinger from under his nose to the corner of his mouth, he wiped off the tomato juice and swept the long mustache hairs out of his mouth. His blue eyes twinkled, and I became aware that he was watch-

Grampa Flansburg.

ing me watch him. I blushed and turned back to my plate and sneaked looks at him. Momma had taught me it wasn't polite to stare.

Grampa was Olin Mattison Flansburg. Most people called him Old Man Flansburg; he said the O. M. stood for Old Man. He was capable and strong with not an ounce of fat on his tall stooped frame. His big hands had seen a lifetime of hard work as a cowboy, farmer, stonemason, dirt mover, and logger.

A barber once told him if he kept his head shaved he'd never go bald, so whenever his hair grew out grizzled to a quarter or half an inch long, he'd have Gramma or one of the grandkids man the hand clippers and haggle it off again.

Grampa made his living with his horses all his life, and he loved his horses. On Thanksgivings when we looked at the family albums, he knew and cared more about the horse pictures than the people pictures. He'd say, "That's old Stinger. Jake got him from that old jigger that lived up by Perma there, oh what'n the hell was his name? I don't know why Jake ever got that horse anyway. I never saw such a son of a bitch ta buck."

Then he'd come to a snapshot of a person. "Who's that, anyway?"

Dad would take a look. "That's old Shorty Thompson up at Stark where we were gettin' out those logs that fall."

Grampa'd adjust his store-bought glasses, tip the picture toward the kerosene lamp, and say, "By God, it is. He had that poppin' good team of sorrels he called Kip and Colley."

This Thanksgiving he got wound up about his early life. He had traveled here to western Montana from Freeport, Illinois, where he was born on June 2nd, 1869. He took the roundabout scenic route through Missouri, Oklahoma Territory, Texas, Canada, Washington, Oregon, and Idaho to what he called God's Country, the Flathead Valley of Montana, specifically in the low, bald Salish hills around Dixon and Perma. Along the way he acquired a wife and nine children.

Grampa was nine years old when his mother died. His father sent him and his two sisters and two brothers to live with their paternal grandmother, who raised them. His father remarried and had seven more children—four boys and three girls.

His grandmother insisted that he become a preacher, and she sent him to a seminary. Was that where he learned all the cuss words he knew? He could swear all day and never repeat himself, but his language was never dirty or offensive like one hears nowadays, unless epithets like "bleary-eyed, blue-bellied, jumped-up Jesus Christ O-mighty!" offends you.

Cuss words were so much a part of his speech that he was honestly unaware he was using them. Mrs. Emma Batey in Dixon tells of the time he was helping her mother, Mrs. Nefner, put in her winter's wood after Mr. Nefner died. Mrs. Nefner mailed a note to Grampa saying that she deeply appreciated his kindness of preparing her wood for winter, but could he please not swear out at the woodpile when her club ladies met at her house. Grampa was contrite and said to her respectfully, "Mrs. Nefner, I'll do my god*damn*dest not to swear around you or your friends anymore."

"I was fourteen when the circus came to town," he told us. He and his seminary friends each got fifty cents to go. One of the circus teamsters was off on a drunk and hadn't shown up to drive one of the horse teams that pulled the fancy circus wagons. The boys watched a novice trying to back up a wagon to unload and not getting the job done. The man in charge called out, "Does anybody here know how to drive a team?"

"Yes!" Grampa answered.

"Can you drive six or eight at a time?"

"I can drive as many as you want to hook up."

"Let's see you back that wagon up to right here."

Grampa did.

"You're hired. Be ready to go tonight."

Grampa hiked back to the seminary, gathered up his few clothes, and wrapped them into a small bundle. At the window of his room he looked out all directions. No one in sight. He dropped his clothes out of the window and walked back to take in the rest of the circus. When it was over he returned to the seminary with his friends. After darkness fell he slipped out, picked up his bundle, and lit out for the circus.

"The Christly graybacks made me quit the circus," he told us. Whenever he drove the circus wagon in parades in his fancy costume, he was supposed to sit up straight and at attention and not move a muscle. It was torture to not be able to squirm while the "graybacks" (lice) chewed on him at will.

Grampa's travels with the circus led him to Texas. Texas! Now that was something like!

"I'll be a Texas cowboy," he told himself, for that looked like a lot more fun than driving a team and wagon at the mercy of the lice. He bought a horse and saddle, a big hat, a pair of chaps, a quirt, and a pair of pointy-toed riding boots and went cowboying.

That usually dry part of Texas was swampy and wet all the time due to the heavy rains of that year. "The only way I could get a dry spot to sleep," he said, "was to dig two trenches and pile the mud up in the middle and roll my bedroll out on that mound. We didn't take our boots off for weeks at a time."

When the job was finished and he finally cut his boots off, his feet were drawn up and hammertoed and compressed by the shrunken boots. The rest of his life he walked flat-footed, painfully stumping along, and he rode a horse if he was going any farther than the barn.

"I damn near got hung in Texas," Grampa said, and he had all the grandkids' attention. He continued.

His boss sent him out to repair fence in a coulee some distance from the ranch buildings. Grampa led his horse along, dropping the reins often to fix the fence. A man galloped up on a horse that was winded and in a lather. The man said, "My wife is dying and I have to get to her! My horse is done for and won't make it."

So Grampa said, "Take mine. For what I'm doin' your horse'll do me."

We sensed the suspense building as Grampa continued his story. "The fella thanks me and pounds off on my horse. He's no more'n outa sight when a posse rides up. All of a goddamn sudden I find myself with a hangman's rope around my neck. The posse's in no mood for explanations."

Here he stopped, dug his curly short-stemmed pipe into his tobacco pouch, and took so long to get it lit that one of us kids prompted, "What happened, Grampa?"

"They hung me."

"No-o. Grampa! What really happened?"

At that moment his boss and two others rode up and convinced the posse that Grampa was his hired hand and had left his ranch to fix fence that very morning.

Years later Dad remembered another one of Grampa's hanging stories, which went this way:

Dad and Grampa were in Bonner, Montana, in the early 1920s looking into a logging job. Dad's brother, Jack, introduced them to his friend Crazy Horse Jack Healy, who could hypnotize a bad horse to make him do anything he wanted him to. Jack Flansburg said Healy had taught him how to do it, and there must have been something to it because Jack could handle any outlaw horse. The catch was you had to be drunk to do it, but that was no problem for Jack Flansburg either.

Upon meeting Healy, in an aside to Dad Grampa says, "You know, I've met that bottle-assed son of a bitch somewhere before, but I can't quite place 'im."

Healy heard him say it, and he got Grampa off to the side. When he told Grampa who he was, Grampa swore never to reveal his real name. In Texas some years before, Healy had sold Grampa a stolen horse. A posse grabbed Grampa, looped a rope around his neck, and was leading his horse up under a stout tree branch when Healy rode up, had the drop on the posse, and made them turn Grampa loose. Grampa took Crazy Horse Healy's outlaw name with him to his grave.

Was either story true? Or were they both true? In any case, something had taken the romance out of being a Texas cowboy, and Grampa drifted back to Missouri.

I never knew how Gramma and Grampa met, but it was most likely in Amsterdam, in Bates County, Missouri, where Gramma grew up. Since she was the retiring, stay-at-home type, that's probably how it happened.

Gramma was Alice Elizabeth Clark, born November 19th, 1869, the daughter of Jack and Elizabeth Clark. Grampa courted her through the mails while he worked in Kansas City, Missouri, as a cable splicer on the Kansas City streetcars and at Armour's meatpacking plant.

His starting job at Armour's was driving the gut wagon, the lowest, stinkingest job there was, but he said, "When you got used to it you could sit right on the wagon and eat your lunch." He graduated to the curing room where sausages and weiners were hooked over racks, then shoved into big smoking-oven rooms. Sometimes sausages would break off around lunch time, "and if they didn't, we'd see that one did," he added dryly.

He told us that Gramma was considered "the belle of the county," and they were married on February 15th, 1893, when they were both twenty-four.

Jack Clark, Grampa's new father-in-law, a little old dried-up plainsman, was an orphan who had been taken by a wagonmaster to the California goldfields in 1848. He went back in 1849 as a guide, this time with teams of oxen. Now he asked his new son-in-law to go with him again, but Mrs. Clark wouldn't let her husband go gallivanting across the continent a third time, so Grampa didn't get to go.

"It sounded like a damn good idea to me. I'd like to of seen that country," Grampa said.

Gramma and Grampa decided to try for a homestead on the free land being offered on the Cherokee Strip in northern Oklahoma Territory. Before noon on April 22nd, 1893, Grampa was among the 20,000 people poised at the starting line. To make it fair, everyone was to start out at the same time. The throng of thousands waited nervously for the soldier to shoot his pistol into the air at exactly twelve noon. About three minutes ahead of time, someone shot off a gun, and with a great shout and a roar, the crowd surged ahead. Men on horseback, men on foot, wagons pulled by oxen or horses, even folks in railroad passenger cars held to going no faster than a horse could run—all raced wildly ahead to find and stake their claim to free land.

Grampa relit his dead pipe, slowly shook out the match, crossed his legs, and asked us, "D'you know why Oklahomans are called 'Sooners'?"

"Why?"

"We all left three minutes too soon."

Grampa staked out a homesite, then returned to register his choice at the land office. Throngs crowded around the office to take a number and wait. Some had waited for days. He said if you stepped out of line for any reason, you lost your place. He stood for less than a day and became so repulsed at people relieving themselves in line so they'd not lose their places that he decided, "The hell with it!" and left the line.

Someone who could get used to eating his lunch while sitting on a gut wagon couldn't have been too squeamish. I suspect it was Gramma who wanted their own piece of land, not Grampa. To pull up stakes and move was hard for her, but for him it was a chance to see more country. Or it may have been that he had to pee, himself, and chose not to do it in the line. Whatever the reason, owning a piece of land was out.

They moved to Missouri, where two sons were born: Zenean Hilton on April 24th, 1894, and Burley Clark on February 3rd, 1896. Some man told Gramma that if she would name her first boy after him, he would buy the baby "the prettiest dress in town." On the strength of that, she tacked "Zenean" on that poor child. Grampa called the boys Jack and Burl.

Grampa continued to hold our attention as he recalled his early days with Gramma. He had been a "dirt stiff" in Missouri and Kansas—that is, he and his teams of horses did dirt work building railroad grades. It was here that Grampa first met the Helean family, who have been in the construction business in Missoula for many years. They did dirt work, too, and Grampa subcontracted road construction work from Buck Helean years later in the Dixon-Perma-Paradise area of Montana.

In the meantime, Gramma and Grampa had moved back to Oklahoma Territory, onto a piece of rented farmland around Tonkawa and Red Rock, where Grampa did dirt moving and harvest work.

Late in May of 1898 Grampa got a job putting up prairie hay several miles from home. The night of June 3rd he crawled into his bedroll under a wagon. As he lay sleeping on the ground he felt the vibration of a horse galloping toward him from a long way off. A man rode up and informed him that his wife had given birth to not one but two brand-new little girls. Gramma named the identical twins Olive Rose and Ollie Artie. Grampa called them Sal and Peg.

Two years later, while still in Red Rock, on January 6th, 1900, Gramma named her next baby Rubye Alice Elizabeth. Grampa called her Midge.

CANADA BECKONS, 1900

A FRIEND NAMED DAN SYLA wrote Grampa from Canada that huge sandstone buildings were going up on the site of the new town of Calgary, and that building was going on at such a clip that half the workers in Calgary in the 1890s were stonemasons. Grampa was a stonemason, and he also had teams of workhorses including his prize Kansas pulling team. He figured he could either work for day labor and get from $1.50 to $2.00 for a ten-hour day, good wages in those days, or he could put his teams to work hauling sandstone to the building sites and make even more money. But to be certain of work when he got there, he got a contract for a haying job on the present site of Calgary through a man named Crawford in Kansas City.

Dan Syla also wrote: "Bring all the oak barrels you can," for he intended to fill them with saskatoons and wild grapes and make wine.

Grampa moved Gramma and their five kids from Red Rock, Oklahoma, back to stay with her parents in Amsterdam, Missouri, until he could get settled and send for them. He began gathering up to go to Canada.

One morning an inconspicuous farm couple drove their team and wagon into Red Rock and put their team up at the blacksmith's. The man stopped in at the harness shop, and the woman went to the drygoods store. They met later at the hardware, then had a bite to eat at the local eatery. They looked in on the Wells Fargo office and sat awhile at the train depot. While the man stepped into the saloon, the woman rested in the lobby of the hotel. They spent all day in town and drove out just before dark.

After dark the "farm couple," now two men on horseback, rode into town to hold up the railway office, the place they had fingered as having the most cash.

Grampa had spent all day at the railway station loading up a boxcar with horses, equipment, the family household goods, and Dan Syla's oak barrels to take to Canada. It was after dark before he finished. He stepped into the railway office just as the two men held it up.

"Stand and deliver!" they barked, then started down the line of people coolly accepting the contents of turned-out pockets and the freight office's cash. They came to Grampa, obviously a filthy, penniless old tramp. They passed him by; they robbed everyone but him. He had on him every cent to their name, enough to get the family to Calgary and then some.

Seventy years later, when Dad and Olive lived alongside each other, Olive brought over a pulp magazine of "true West" stories.

"Remember Dad telling us about meeting up with the Mother Hubbard Gang?" she asked Dad. In the magazine was an account of how the Mother Hubbard Gang operated in Kansas and Oklahoma Territory around the turn of the century.

Grampa left Red Rock riding in the boxcar so he could look after his horses. From Calgary he wrote for Gramma and the five kids to come. Among the two large sacks of old letters Gramma had saved over her lifetime, I found her reply.

Amsterdam, Mo.
April 28. 1901.

My dear Olin

Your long looked for letter was recieved a week ago and Should have been answard befour now but I did notknow how to answer I did not want to write that I would come and then not get off the children have all been sick but are better now but are awful fretful I don't think it best to start by myself I know I would be plum tired out. I think you had better come back hear I feel sure I would not like it there and don't want to come atall come back and try for a claim in the New Country [central Oklahoma Territory] it is going to be opened with a draw. I wish you would come back and we would go down in the strip right away and work throw harvest. but if you don't come I am going down with the rest of the folks and make a draw the one that draws Number 1 gets first chiose of the hole country. now who knows but what I might be that lucky one. . . but if you would rather I would come thair I will come thow I would much rather you would come back hear O: I do wish I was with you to night the childern all want to see Papa very much. . . Please let me hear from you at once from Alice

His answer has been mouse chewed, but enough remains to tell us he wrote it from Calgary on May 5th, 1901.

> *. . . You must be craisy to think of going to that opening they would not let you draw if you were there and . . . they don't let anyone draw unless it is the head of a family. . . you musn't take too much stock in what sheets [Frank Sheets, his brother-in-law] says about this cuntry he did not see any of it to speak of it is a pretty good place to make money and we are making some to in spite of having to batch and buy feed for all the stock. . .*

I puzzle out all that's left of another letter to Gramma. It seems Grampa was encouraging Bill (Gramma's brother) to come up and work for him and probably to help Gramma get there with the kids.

> *. . . 1000 tons and we will get $2.50 or $3.00 a ton acording to the sise of the grass we don't know what waidges will be yet but expect to pay $2.00 a day and board for men we have to hire if he will come he will make more money counting out his B & B fare than he will by working down there all summer he must tell Crawford he intends to take up a quarter of land out here so he will get a cheap rate fare and you must have him see after getting your tickets for you and don't forget to keep the boys age under 5 you might get Zene through if Bill is with you Do as Crawford thinks best about him [Zene (Jack) was now 7.] be sure and write 2 or 3 days ahead what time you will stop I will send you $1500 and more but won't have it to spare till pay day and that is the first of the month [June 1st] well kiss all the babies and tell them papa is dieing to see them. good Bie Olin*

But Bill didn't go. Gramma was terrified to go so far away alone. Grampa wrote further instructions and more encouragement to come.

> *. . . have Rosa [Gramma's sister] meet you at KC [Kansas City] and go to Crawford's office and he will fix you up all right and you won't have any trouble if you just think so. If you don't like it here we will pull out the first of Sept and go south west but this is a pretty good place to live it is good and helthy and cooll and nice wood is cheap we got a $1.00 worth when we first came here and have a good deal left yet and it was already cut stove length and most of it is small enough for the stove we eat Beef 3 times a day boiling beef is .05 cts a lb. so we have all we want. You had better pack up and come right away and let me know what day you will start so I can meet you at the train. kiss all the babies for me and yourself to.*
>
> *Olin*

Gramma followed instructions. She boarded the Immigration Train at Kansas City, Missouri, and left for Canada, just herself and the children. This had to have been the most frightening time of her entire life. She had never been anywhere alone before. Now she faced 1,200 miles alone with five small children under the age of seven. Midge was in diapers; it is possible the twins were, too; plus she had two wiggly boys of five and seven.

Gramma had a lifelong habit of keeping something in her mouth between her teeth and her cheek. Somewhere along the way to Canada their train pulled out from a station and got a ways down the track when she choked on a straight pin while changing a diaper. The conductor pulled the cord, stopped the train, and told the engineer of the emergency. He backed the train up to the station they had just left, Gramma got medical attention, and in a few minutes she reboarded the train and away they went.

Farther on down the track she discovered Jack was missing! They searched the train. No Jack. The engineer backed up the train again to the same station, and they all looked for him there. Still no Jack. It seemed there was nothing to do but to go on. At the next station a man picked up his coat off the floor to leave the train. There lay Jack sound asleep curled up on the floor under the man's coat.

Drawing on strength she never knew she had, Gramma made it to Calgary with herself and her five kids intact.

When I knew Gramma in the 1930s, '40s, and '50s she was timid and retiring. She talked fast but so soft and low, scarcely allowing the words to leave her throat, that it was hard to hear her, and unless I read her lips and listened closely I had trouble understanding her. Did she think that what she had to say was unimportant? Or had she been taught to speak very softly in order to be "ladylike"? Certainly she was raised in an age when only males were supposed to have the opinions, and women were subservient. She had been sent to "finishing school," whatever that amounted to then, so she could learn to write with the flourishes and fancy penmanship that signified "good breeding."

Gramma wore a black velvet band around her neck all of her life. When her grandkids asked, "Gramma, why do you always wear that around your neck?" she intimated it was to prevent goiter, but she was a vain old gal, and most likely it was a beauty thing. I saw her only once

Gramma Flansburg.

without the band, when I was seven or eight and she came to our house overnight. She slept with me, and getting ready for bed that night she took it off. Kidlike, I stared and bluntly asked, "Gramma, why do you wear that thing?" She gave me some noncommital answer, probably figuring I was getting too personal.

Appearance was important to her. Her Smith grandkids who lived with her in the '30s say that whenever someone came to the door, she'd run to the bedroom and hide; then later she would come out smiling with white powder on her cheeks. She was a very long time turning gray; she used coffee on her hair. No one ever saw Gramma without her false teeth. She kept a little metal dish on the back of the wood cookstove in which she put candles, old broken cylinder phonograph records—

anything that would melt. Her grandkids asked, "What's that black stuff for?" "Never mind" was her answer. They learned much later that she used it to hold in her false teeth.

When she was young and having babies, Gramma held straight pins in her mouth. Later she kept a button between her teeth and her cheek "to hold the false teeth in." Her mouth was always moving, always working, as if she kept hard candy or some such in her mouth, but it was the button.

My dad was born in Calgary on February 8th, 1904. Gramma named him Lelan Lawrence. Grampa called him Jim.

Grampa bought more teams and wagons and worked them in the stone quarries in the winters. In summers he contracted haying jobs from a man named Patrick Burns, who was one of the four men who financed the first Calgary Stampede in 1912. One winter Grampa fed and herded bull oxen on the Bar U Ranch. They were prospering in Calgary. Gramma even had a cook and a maid.

Then one cold winter Grampa freighted coal into Calgary for a light plant using four horses on a bobsled hauling five to six tons per load over the ice. He left way early in the mornings and unloaded late at night in fifty-below-zero weather. He worked all winter on this job and was never paid for it. This may have been the beginning of prosperity's departure.

They moved a few miles south of Calgary to Okatoks, where Gramma delivered another boy on March 27th, 1905. She named him Darrell Donavan. Grampa called him Jake.

In the sacks of Gramma's old letters is this one, typical of her mother's many letters to her, postmarked May 11th, 1909.

> *My Dear Daughter Alice it is with grate pleasure that I take my pen in hand to endever to ancer your most kind and verrywelcome but long looked for letter which came to hand a fiew days a go and I cant begin to tell you how glad I was to get it for I had almost begin to think I nevr wood here from you a gane and I hope you wont ever be so long a gaine for it makes me so werried and feel so lonesome I would love to get a letter every week but if I get one every month it wouldent be so bad I know you have lots to doe with a big familey but your childern is big enouf to help you lots and I think they might write a letter once and a while eney way I think you doe well to cook for five men but it makes lots of work I know. Oh Alice I want*

to see you all So bad I cant hardley stand it I would be so glad to see [you] I dont know what I would doe I beleve I would feel ten years younger Alice I doe wish you would come home cant you come this fall and stay all winter I would love to have you stay a year I wish you would all come back and stay but I dont guess you ever think of that Alice doe you like to live out ther Dou you think it is a better country to live in than this I doe want to see you So bad if I could I would go see you but I cant but I think you could come to see me I know it is a long waye out thare and it cost a good bit to come but oh it would doe me So much good to see you and the childern and Olin but I am afraid I never will see you a gaine in this World but hope that we will all meet in a nather and better World where thare will be No more parting and No sad farwells but oh I would be so glad to see you be fore I die.

And on and on . . .

Some shysters convinced Grampa he could do well in British Columbia. Grampa was a flatlander who knew very little about mountain terrain at that time. The fellows showed him a tiny patch of timber from all four sides, and he believed them when they said it was a big patch. He moved the family to his new venture near Creston, British Columbia.

In short order he realized he'd been had, but to finish up the job he mortgaged his Kansas pulling team to a bank in Calgary. He lost his shirt. When the bank came to get his beloved team, he gave them a team that matched their description, then he gathered up his belongings, his seven kids, and his pregnant wife, and overnight he pulled his freight for the border fifteen miles away.

At Port Hill, Idaho, where they paused briefly to catch their breath, Gramma wrote her mother in Missouri that they were back in the United States.

BACK IN THE U.S.A., 1909

I ALWAYS FIGURED I'd find my shirt where I lost it," Grampa said, "and that would be in another loggin' job."

So after a stint of dirt work on a large irrigation project near Prosser, Washington, Grampa moved the family to Elgin, in the logging country of northwest Oregon along the Grande Ronde River Valley. He didn't work there long, and it could be because he was wiser about picking his logging jobs.

In Elgin on April 5th, 1909, Gramma had their eighth child, a girl whom she named Azalia Myrtle. Grampa called her Zale.

Zale contracted polio at two years old and became crippled and walked with a built-up shoe all her life. She couldn't dance, but she could play fluent ragtime on the piano and make her brothers and sisters dance their shoes off. Dad said when Zale played the piano you couldn't stand still—you just had to dance. After Dad was crippled his main grief was that he wouldn't be able to dance again.

While the rest of the family stayed in Elgin, Grampa, Jack, and Burl (now 16 and 14) went to Yakima to work on dirt- and rock-moving jobs. In spite of all the work Gramma had to do caring for her large family she was lonesome for her husband whenever he worked miles from home. She must have written asking him to come home. I find this letter that Grampa writes to Gramma:

Jan 26, 1911

. . . We get $4.85 a team and all 4 teams at work so you can see we cant come home just now. . . Be careful of the baby [Zale] and tell her I am coming home some day Kiss all of them for me yourself included

Olin

Another letter reads:

Dear Alice and children I have not heard from you for over a week you never told me if you got my checque or not but I guess you got it or you would have been hollering for money. We are still working for the dagos we will get done today or tomorrow. . . . let me know if the sign is right and I will come down next saturday if it is kiss all the kids for me love to all

Olin

Apparently "the sign" was right, for while they were in their next home in Sprague, Washington, Gramma awaited the birth of their last child.

After another dirt-moving job in Sprague, Grampa and Burl left for Coeur d'Alene, Idaho, to hunt up a good logging job. Their correspondence continued. Gramma's time of confinement was drawing near. She wrote:

Sprague Wash.
Feb 20, 1912

My dear Olin and Burley,

it has been a long time since you have wrote to us I have been looking and looking for a letter from you till I cant wait any longer Olin I want you and Burley to come home just as soon as you can get here I am liabel to need you any time and bring a nurse with you if you can possibly get one for you cant get one here. they havent got but two at the hospitle one day and one night nurse and there is no one else to get. I have got a Girl engaged I guess she will be heare next Monday. I hope you and Burley can be here by Saturday. I want Burley to be sure to come with you for I want to see him awful bad the childern are all well I think little Azalia can walk quite a lot better than she did when you wase here. she talks a lot about you and Burley Well I must close and get to doing something Olive Ollie Ruby & Lelen are at school Zeney went out in the country to day with Elmer Smith. . . . Darley and little Azalia are playing out on the front porch. Well I will quite now hopeing to see you both in a few days

Your loving wife and mother Alice Flansburg

Grampa wrote back the next day.

Chatcolet Feb 21 1912

Dear Alice yours recieved today have been looking for a letter for a long time. I will be home Sunday night if I can make connections all right Burl cant come till I get back here again we have got to keep things going here all the time or go in the hole and we cant do that. . . . Love to all Olin

Grampa went home to Sprague, then wrote when he got back to the Idaho job:

> *Dear Alice I am sending you $25.00 let me know when you get it and how you are it is a good job I came back there was nothing doing here they had not skidded a log and only hauled a fiew. Kiss the babies for me Love to all Olin*

On March 4th, 1912, four days before the baby was born, Grampa wrote this letter:

> *Dear Alice I have not had time to write and ought to be in bed now the sleighing is about gone and we are trying to get everything out we can before it goes if you need me tellegraph to Harrison and have them phone to Chatcolet or Conklings there well be a phone ther in a fiew days We are well but getting aughfull tired Love to all Olin*

On March 8th, 1912, Gramma delivered her ninth and last child, a girl. Had Grampa received word in time to get there? He, himself, named this new baby Dulce Eulala. But he called her Dutch.

Years later someone asked Gramma why they never had any more children, and she snapped, "I got a recipe."

LARCENY, 1939

DURING THE DEPRESSION a dollar was worth one long day's work, if you could get work. Fanny Hughes helped my mother in the kitchen on days there was too much work for one woman to do. Canning and haying seasons came at the same time, and the pressure-canner gauge had to be watched and the gas pumps attended at the same time, along with the usual housework and errands. At the end of one of those long, hard day's work Mom gave Fanny the going wage, one silver dollar, then gave her a ride home.

My father made the family living any way he could. In his shop at the garage he did repair work on vehicles or farm machinery and sold gas and oil and tires. He had a wrecker service and was on call day and night. He had the bus run to the Clinton grade school. The nickels came hard.

Mom on the high lope headed for Missoula on a parts run. She wrote on the back of this picture, "In a tearing hurry! (the usual pace)."

I was a gangly girl, all legs like a colt, and had reddish blonde hair cut in a becoming short shingle. I hated my hair. I was a romantic. What I really wanted were two long black braids hanging down my back like pictures of beautiful dark-skinned Indian maidens, but no such luck.

When I was ten years old, the 1939 Christmas edition of the Sears & Roebuck catalog arrived in the mail. I took possession of it and curled up on the front-room davenport that Grampa Mueller had made from the good back seat of a wrecked car. I turned to the toy section and began to dream.

I turned the pages looking for balls and jump ropes. Dolls were nice, but what could you do with them except park them in a corner to watch while you read stories? Dolls were only inside companions and not very communicative at that.

My eyes lit on a page of small girl-size furniture. These kinds of toys I'd never even considered before. There was the cutest little play cookstove, not like Mom's old black wood cookstove, but an electric one with big and little round burners painted on. It was one of those new kinds like in the big stove section that had legs, and the oven side was taller than the cooking side. I could visualize play salt and pepper shakers and pretty potholders on top of that oven.

On the next page was a darling little play-like electric icebox just like Mom's new one she had bought secondhand from Walkers when they moved from the Milwaukee substation at Ravenna. Hers was the latest kind, a big white box with legs and a little round top on it that looked like a round head on a square snowman.

Slowly I turned the page to some small tables and chairs. "I don't need those," I said aloud. I still had the set that Grampa Mueller built, one for me and one for my cousin Florence.

There were several choices of play dishes and pots and pans to outfit my little kitchen, hard choices because they were all so cute. I turned the page. There was a toy ironing board with an electric play iron, and a girl with long black braids was smiling and ironing in the picture.

I felt as if I were seeing girl toys for the first time, and I was enchanted.

Mom came hurrying into the front room to make change for a sale at the gas pumps. The left top drawer of the buffet was the change drawer, "the money drawer" we called it. Carefully counting it out, she shut the

My cousin Florence Dufresne (left) and me among Gramma Mueller's day lilies. She was my favorite playmate, and we often stayed together at our grandparents' ten-acre place on Seventh Street in Orchard Homes.

drawer, turned the key in the lock, dropped the key in the drawer next to it, and went out to give the customer his change. Then she went back to cooking supper.

"Yes, they're very nice," Mom said when I showed her all the lovely toys in the small hope she would buy them. There was no guarantee at all that I would ever have them. I had leaped from never even thinking of toys like these to *needing* them. *All* of them. And I was sick and tired of being told, "Well, we can't buy anything like that right now, but you will have a nice Christmas."

Self-pity took over. Every day after school I mooned over those toy pages and bemoaned my penniless state. Here I was, in the fifth grade and no money. My nickel-a-week allowance would buy five pieces of penny candy. A loaf of Eddy's bread was a nickel, too, in this year of 1939, but I did not have to spend my allowance on things like bread. It was nearly impossible to save up enough to buy even a twenty-five-cent scrapbook for movie star pictures because of Mrs. Milward's candy counter.

Once in a great while my best friend, Louella Hesselgesser, and I strolled down to Mrs. Milward's store at noon hour where we pressed our noses against her curved display case. While we pondered how to get the most for the least, Mrs. Milward waited with her arm propped up on the counter, chin in her hand, eyes locked on some point on the opposite wall. After we made our decision we wandered back to the school yard, munching our treats slowly to make them last, and waited our turn to get on the teeter-totter, our favorite fun.

I added up the prices of my toy choices. At $10.38 I knew the hard reality of it: I'd never be able to save up enough money to get my toys. I already considered them *my* toys. I could never be happy unless I got that cunning little kitchen furniture. Feeling sorry for myself set me up for the boldness to take what was "rightfully" mine because I deserved it. No one need ever know!

A plan was the next thing. No one ever kept watch over the money drawer, so each day I began to take small pieces of change, never paper money or silver dollars, for they would be missed. But dimes were good and once in a while a fifty-cent piece or a quarter. Indian-head pennies and nickels, too, because there were more of them than anything else. Daily I selected a very few coins and stored my stash in the most ingenious place—inside the bottom of the piano! Anyone could walk by the piano all day and never know there was a growing pile of money in there.

I made out my order, writing carefully and adding it several times. When it totaled $10.38 three times in a row, I was ready. . . . Wait! That didn't include the postage it asked for at the bottom of the page. It seemed that so many "lbs" and "oz" would cost so much postage. This meant I had to add up all the lbs and oz's and figure how much extra that would add up to. I laboriously calculated how much more change would be needed. Had this been an arithmetic problem in school, I'd have vowed I couldn't do it, but the necessity made it quite possible. Not easy, but possible. I took out that amount over the next two days. Plus a little more in case I had overlooked something else.

I borrowed a three-cent stamped envelope from Mom's stationery supplies, and another one without a stamp on it to carry the money in. I was ready.

At noon the next school day I walked straight to the Clinton Post Office. No friends were invited this time, and I ate no lunch from my lunch bucket until I got back. Ethel Peers, the postmistress, calmly counted out my envelope full of change. Although it was my first business dealing of that sort, I was sure I had carried it off like a pro, for Mrs. Peers didn't ask anything I couldn't answer.

The deed was done. That day after school I replaced the few cents that were left over from my transaction. There was no use to *steal*, for heaven sakes.

And then I forgot about it.

Three weeks passed by quickly.

One morning Dad's longtime friend Eric Freudenreich was headed for the post office and offered to pick up our mail as well. He came struggling up the sidewalk lugging a huge box. In that frozen moment I grew wide-eyed and put a hand to my mouth. It had never entered my mind what would happen when my toys came, for I had never looked any further than the ordering. My skin prickled with hot shame, and I was mute with fear.

Mom opened the door for Eric saying, "Well, I wonder what this could be." Eric jockeyed the awkward box between the doorjambs and set it on the front-room floor. Mom opened the box. Play dishes? Small stove, icebox, ironing board? Who had sent these things? Was there some mistake in the address? "Lois Flansburg, Box 43, Clinton, Montana. . . . Oh-h-h," Mom intoned.

It all came out. And right in front of Eric. I thought, "Why did he have to see my most shameful moment? Why couldn't he have just put the box down and left? No, he had to wait around to see what was in it and watch me squirm and turn red." I hated him! He might tell Dad, and Dad didn't just get mad—he got awful mad. I felt sick thinking of his wrath.

When Eric finally left, I whispered miserably to Mom, "Don't tell Dad."

"Well, he'll have to know sometime. But until there's money to send them back, we'll store this in the attic."

"Why can't you take it out of the money drawer?"

"That's not our money. It belongs to Hart Refinery. We get two cents for every gallon of gas we sell. We would have to sell about six hundred gallons of gas to pay for all of these toys, but certainly not that much to pay the return postage."

Each day for the next week I crawled up into the attic to where the box sat among the stored squashes. I took out the little iron and ironing board and cried over them.

The box was mailed back. I got no allowance until the postage money was paid back, and except for that, it seemed to Mom that my pain had already been sufficient to deter future crimes of this sort.

It took three weeks to gather up the return postage, and those three weeks crept by ever so slowly. As each miserable day dawned, I wondered, "Will this be the day that Dad finds out what I've done?" When I had accidently fallen from the moving car, he had spanked me hard, no doubt from relief I wasn't killed, a concept I would not understand until I had children of my own. And when I had cried because I thought the hired men were going to eat my birthday cake I had baked for my party, he had spanked me long and hard. I never understood why these things were so bad, but I had been punished rather severely nonetheless. This time I *knew* what I had done wrong.

If Dad ever did find out about my thievery, I never knew it, but my fear became honed to a sharp point by the spanking I had earned but never got.

ALONE, 1940

HURRY! RUN GET YOUR DAD! The baby has convulsions!" called Mom. I raced in my pajamas barefoot through the snow to the barn where Dad was milking.

Rex was five and I was eleven when Mom was going to have another baby. "Around the end of May after school is out," she said. I leaned over the Singer treadle and watched her hem up three dozen soft diapers and make a dozen kimonos from a delicate flower print of peach outing flannel.

She let me pick out the set of clothes to bring the new baby home. I chose a peach kimono, a bellyband, a tiny white shirt, a pair of tiny white booties, an outing flannel blanket, and diapers. "Better put in three or four diapers 'just in case,' " she advised. I packed the baby things on top of Mom's things in her small black suitcase with the blue lining, the one she'd had since she was in teachers' normal school in Dillon.

The day came. Dad took Rex and me to Orchard Homes to stay with Mom's folks, Gramma and Grampa Mueller; then he drove Mom to St. Pat's Hospital in Missoula.

The next evening he came back saying we had a new little brother, and he took us to see Mom in a room with six other women who had new babies. She had heard Dad's bum leg thumping up the hall, and she was expecting us. It had taken her a long time to have the baby, and she looked awfully tired. She smiled and remarked to Dad, "I don't have the hip bones for this job, Jim."

As we left, Dad said, "We're gonna celebrate!" He took us to the Pallas Candy Shop, an ice cream parlor next to the Wilma Theater. We were impressed. Much as we loved Mom's mush bowls of homemade, freezer-cranked ice cream with all the crushed, sweetened fresh strawberries you cared to pile on it, we felt royally treated to eat "town ice cream" out of little short-stemmed silver cups with dainty long-handled spoons. We sat at the counter on tall, red-padded stools with short wire backs, eating and listening to Dad joshing with the Greek proprietor.

Mom, Rex, and our baby.

He was in a fine mood celebrating his new boy, and we knew May 31st was one special day.

A week later when Mom and Baby George came home, Rex and I got to see our baby for the first time. He had a big soft bump about an inch and a half high on the back of his head. I asked, "What's that thing?" Mom explained, "It's fluid under the scalp from taking so long to be born. It won't hurt him. The doctor says it will eventually disappear."

We lived in the country with no playmates closer than Clinton two miles away. We three were each others' playmates and best friends. At five and a half months old, little George was "just as big as the big kids."

Rex, Baby George, and me. My Big Tree is just above my head in this picture.

His pink lips formed "o-o-o's" as he talked to us, and when he told a *really* exciting story, he waved and kicked his arms and legs at high speed. We three spent hours talking and laughing, each of us taking delight in our two favorite playmates.

Rex held the safety pins while I learned to change diapers. Just the wet ones. Mom did the others.

We took long walks on warm summer days. Rex and I took turns pushing Baby George in his tall wicker buggy. We went out past the gas pumps to the shop to visit Dad; out around the barn and hayshed to see Creamy, the milk cow, and Dan, Dad's big bay saddlehorse; then back around by the icehouse, the woodshed, and the root cellar; past the bunkhouse and the outhouse. Then we swung by Mom's acre of garden, then back underneath the clothesline trees to the house.

It was fun to watch Baby George and Dad play together. Dad set him on the thigh of his good left leg where the baby gently jounced as Dad tapped his heel on the floor and sang "deedle-deedle-dee" lyrics to "Turkey in the Straw," ending with "Bump! Diddledy-de-ump-bump! Bump! Bump!" Or Dad would close one eye and "clk, clk, clk" with his tongue in his cheek, and he and Baby George would smile at each other with glee.

Rex and I stood close by when Dad held and cuddled our baby. To hang around close was the next best thing to being held yourself, and we had grown too big to be held. When Rex was small Dad had held him like that. My favorite picture of Dad and me is when I was around a year old. He is sitting outside on a seat made from the back seat of a wrecked car. His bum leg is crossed over his good one and sticks out straight with its stiff knee. He is holding me up, and we are grinning into each other's faces. I know he held me once, for that picture proves it. When did I get too big to be held and cuddled?

I knew in my knower that both Mom and Dad loved and enjoyed us three kids in spite of working every day to dog-tiredness to make a living in Depression times and keep up with the daily chores. They never quarreled with each other (that we knew of anyway) and were companionable with us and included us in their conversations, but in our family we didn't kiss or touch or embrace each other. I had an idea that Mom and Dad kissed after they went to bed at night, for I often

My favorite picture of Dad and me.

heard soft, unintelligible murmurings from the front room where they slept, but they showed no touching-type of affection toward each other in the daytime.

One time just before Dad swung up on Dan to leave with his pack string for a week-long elk-hunting trip over on the South Fork, he embraced Mom and kissed her right in front of us kids. I felt surprised and warmed and embarrassed.

Kissing was a foreign thing to me, even at a very young age; we didn't even touch. No patting or holding hands or a friendly arm draped across the shoulder. Our family's Scotch-Irish, German, and Dutch blood ran either hot or cold with nothing in between.

By fall Baby George was nearly six months old, and his bump was beginning to go down.

One Sunday morning in mid-November I awoke early and padded out to the cold front room. The banked fire in the coal heater had gone out in the night. I saw Mom as she first leaned over the baby's crib. She cried out, "Oh my God!" Little George was in convulsions. His bluish little body was bent backward, bowed out with head and heels on one side and tummy protruding the opposite direction in an arc. He was unconscious, and his mouth and fingers twitched of their own accord.

"Run get Jim! He's milking!"

Dad limped back to the house in double time. "Get him in warm water!" he ordered. But the fire in the kitchen cookstove had been out since late the evening before and had not yet been started, so neither the reservoir nor the hot water tank yielded any warm water.

Dad ordered me to get some kindling. I ran to the woodshed, but in my numbed state I couldn't find any. Dad came out quickly and began to pick up small chips and sticks, urging, "Hurry up with this kindling! That baby might die!" The resulting panic rendered me blind to anything resembling kindling.

Dad hurried on into the house and started both fires. Then he raced the old Ford the two miles to the Clinton Store, which had the only phone around, and called Dr. Turman, who drove the twenty miles in his "Old Gray Goose" in record time.

Mom sent me to the nearest neighbor, a quarter mile away, for a bucket of warm water. I ran all the way, fell into Mrs. Dyerman's opened door, and began to sob, finally becoming coherent enough to wail, "I gotta have warm water! Baby George is gonna die!" That kind lady drew my bucket full and one of hers and took us back in her car, arriving right behind the doctor.

The doctor stayed all that day and night. When Gramma Mueller arrived to stay with Rex and me the next morning, Dr. Turman had the folks take our baby to St. Pat's Hospital.

It was a long day. That night Gramma slept with me. I awoke sometime in the dark of the night and went into the front room. Mom and Dad were in bed asleep.

"How's the baby?"

No answer. They must be asleep.

I crawled back into bed and asked Gramma, "How's the baby?"

She answered gently, "They couldn't save him. He died."

Gramma Mueller, Baby George, Rex, and me.

I fell asleep sobbing as she held me in the crook of her arm.

The funeral was on a cold, dreary, overcast day in November. Mom's sister Mildred took bewildered little Rex with her into the big part of the funeral home, while Mom and Dad and I were ushered into the little room they called the family room. I could see the little white casket from where I sat beside Dad. Mom sat on the other side of Dad weeping silently, covering her face with a white handkerchief. Dad slumped in his chair staring blankly at some point on the floor in front of him. Bouquets of chrysanthemums gave off their sickly sweet funeral smell. Somebody sang a sad song. The service droned on.

Then, as an organ played quietly in the background, the people in the big room filed past the little coffin. Some people wouldn't look; a few went up close; most only glanced over as they passed by looking sad. When the long procession ended, we in the family room were supposed to go up and see him. Rex came up with Mildred, and he wandered into Dad's way. "God dammit, Rex! Get outta the way!" snapped Dad, and kicked at him with the side of his bum leg. Immediately Mildred got hold of Rex's hand and gently led him off to the other side.

Our baby lay with his hands up by his head in peaceful slumber. As we stood watching his silent sleep, Dad suddenly burst into wrenching, wracking sobs. It frightened me! My eleven-year-old mind thought it was all right for men to get mad, but men weren't supposed to cry. I felt alone with no one to lean on.

We were led out into the cold, gloomy late afternoon. The sky was a leaden gray, and it looked like it would snow soon. Mom and Dad and I were guided into the funeral home's black limousine. Mom still wept silently, hidden in her handkerchief. Dad sat in the middle, his head bowed, eyes closed, holding the bridge of his nose. I reached over and patted his arm in a timid gesture of sympathy. There was no reaction.

Our black limousine followed the one ahead that carried our baby to the cemetery. Slowly we descended into the Orange Street Underpass. And as the black cars oozed through the long stretches of inky blackness between two small bars of light, that dark tunnel became a horror.

I was alone. Stark alone.

Time stopped, and I remember no more of that day.

Neither Mom or Dad ever spoke of Baby George again.

RAGE, 1941

DAD STUMPED INTO THE HOUSE, the boot on his bum leg hitting the floor hard. He flung open the gun cabinet and ordered:

"Go run in the saddlehorse!"

I hot-footed it out to the pasture wondering why he was in such a hurry to get to the hills. If he were going anywhere else he'd take the car. And why in such a hurry? Was a cougar bothering his cattle? It wasn't to kill a deer because he was too mad. Besides it was summer and not hunting season, though that never stopped him from getting meat if we needed it.

Dan, Dad's big, tall, bay saddlehorse, was clear up in the wide end of the three-cornered pasture. He decided that day he would play instead of going to the corral. I could see that this was one day I needed to get Dan corralled in a hurry, and that silly old fool was going to give me trouble. The chase became game time for him and dogged determination for me. I ran him back and forth across the wide end, then yelled and threw rocks at him as he cantered toward the pointy end where I wanted him to go through the gate. He a-a-almost got there, then doubled back and raced past me with his black tail held high. Damn him anyway! Dad was in a mood to give me a lickin' if I didn't get this fool horse in right now, and he picked today to give me trouble.

Back I went, and we repeated the process until *he* decided he'd had his play for the day and trotted into the corral nice as you please. I shut the gate behind him, called him a dirty old son of a bitch, and dog-trotted to the house.

"Dan's in, Dad!"

"Turn 'im loose."

I stood with my mouth open. Had I heard that right?

"I said, turn 'im loose!"

What was going on here? Dad was slumped in his big chair with his hand across his forehead propping his head up, looking emotionally spent. Mom was sitting quietly nearby.

I sauntered back out to the corral, opened the gate, and violently pitched a clod at Dan's retreating rump. It hit him with a splatter, and he farted and ran full tilt for freedom. All that grief for nothing. And after running my guts out, too.

I ambled back to the house taking the long way around. I was curious but I knew better than to barge into their discussion. Things were tense in there.

Rex was out on top of the root cellar when I came by. He had a highway construction job going on the cellar and was skillfully guiding a toy truck along a mountain road. He was uneasy today and not as dedicated to his trucking job as he usually was.

"Dad's awful mad about somethin'," he told me.

"Yeah," I answered. We were both subdued. When Dad got mad, you didn't want to be the cause of it. You also wanted to avoid being around if he was mad at somebody else.

"I'm hungry," Rex said. When he was nervous he ate; when I was nervous I couldn't swallow. We slipped into the kitchen, and I began to fix him a peanut butter sandwich. Mom calmly said to us, "Get your jackets and walk down the railroad right-of-way to Gramma and Grampa Mueller's now. We'll pick you up this evening."

The top of this old root cellar was the place of Rex's early excavations and logging jobs. Behind it is the bunkhouse where Ted lived.

We walked the two miles to their new place at the west end of Clinton. This whole thing was beyond our six- and twelve-year-old minds. "What do you suppose is going on?" we asked each other. Neither of us could imagine, but we were glad to be out of Dad's way.

Over the next few days we learned that Dad had intended to kill the hired man.

Ted had worked for Dad for a long time. He lived in our little one-man bunkhouse out under the clothesline trees. That little bunkhouse used to be the bathhouse at the Old Place's tourist court. Its bright orange paint had weathered off to a mottled brindle. A nine-by-twelve-foot linoleum rug just nicely fit, and it held all the comforts of home, counting the WPA outhouses out back of the shop. There was a little wood heater with a place to stack a few chunks of wood and kindling, and a single bed with plenty of quilts. The washstand held a bucket of water and a gray enamel washbasin. Above it were a mirror and towel rack. Nails were the clothes closet.

Ted and Dad were friendly; he even went with Dad one fall on his annual elk-hunting trip into the South Fork. Ted's sister and her kids rented the house on Dad's Starvation Creek place. That house sat at the mouth of the gulch between two steep mountains.

I once overheard Dad telling Mom that Ted had been sloughing off a lot lately: "He thinks he has a 'position' instead of a job."

That day Ted's job was to pick rocks off a field and dump them over a bank up by the house. While Dad plowed nearby in a gumbo field with four horses on a gang plow, he saw that Ted's team and wagon hadn't moved all afternoon from where he had parked them up by his sister's house.

As the afternoon wore on Dad became enraged. "No rocks picked and I'm payin' for him to sit at his sister's kitchen table drinkin' coffee all day!" He unhooked the plow, and riding on one horse he took his team up to the house and headed for the barn.

Ted sauntered out onto the porch, chewing on a toothpick, and chirped, "Yer quittin' early today, huh?"

Dad shook a menacing finger at Ted and answered, "Just as soon as I take care-a these horses, I'll be back and take care-a you!"

Ted didn't wait to see what "take care-a you" meant. He took off straight up the steep mountainside knowing Dad was crippled and couldn't follow him. Dad swore he'd track him down and shoot him.

While I was out running Dan in, Mom talked him down out of some of his blind rage: "Jim, until you can use your head again, you'll have to use mine." She was only partly successful.

Dad gave up the idea of running him down in the hills. Instead he put the .30/.30 rifle in the front seat of the old '34 Ford and drove back to the ranch house in case Ted had doubled back. But Ted was nowhere in sight. Ted's sister and Dad talked a long while. She said, "I know he hasn't done you right, Jim, but please don't shoot him."

That evening Dad came to pick us up. The .30/.30 still lay in the front seat of the car. He had spent all afternoon driving up and down the road looking for Ted to emerge from the hills. Before we got in, Dad pumped the shells out of it, and we drove home.

Ted had left the country. His nephew smuggled him out. They had relatives somewhere in Colorado, so it's likely he went there. At least that's what people say. No one around here ever saw him again.

MY LIFE WITH HORSES

AT TWELVE YEARS OLD my future was decided. "A rodeo trick rider! That's what I'll be!"

Down the arena she came, arms straight above her head, standing on the saddle of her white horse as he galloped past the grandstand where we sat. She wore slim-fitting white pants and a white blouse with green sparkly lapels and cuffs. Her full sleeves fluttered behind her arms as she sped by. Next she vaulted from side to side over her horse as he ran past us. People applauded. I sat open-mouthed in worship, too awed to clap my hands.

"Yessir. A trick rider is what I'll be."

My first rodeo the summer of 1941 was the last one until World War II ended. That first one was so exciting because Dad sat beside me telling me all about the rules of the game. His enthusiasm was contagious.

"Daddy, why does that guy hold his hand up high like that?"

"The bronc rider can only hang on with one hand, and the other one can't touch the horse at any time. If it does he's disqualified."

Out bounced another horse and rider from a chute, and Dad pointed out, "See how the rider raked his spurs from the horse's neck to his flanks on the first jump outa the chute? He'll get points for that."

"What's points?"

"See those two riders off a ways on either side? They're the judges, and they watch how good his ride is. Each judge gives him so many points for how he makes his ride. They add 'em together and that's his score."

During the next wild ride Dad clapped and yelled, "Waa-a-a hoo!" at the good performance, and then he told me why it was good. "D'ju see how that horse swapped ends and turned his belly up to the sun with every jump? That's called sunfishin'. The rider's stirrups touch the ground on both sides. That was a helluva ride! That's one'a the best rides I ever saw. Waa-a-a hoo!" And he clapped his big hands together to make lots of noise. I did too.

After seeing cowboys ride sunfishers, calf roping seemed pretty tame to me until Dad said, "Watch how that horse works, honey. He's lookin' right down that rope, pullin' back just enough to keep the rope tight while the roper ties three loops an' a dally. When he throws his hands in the air like that, it tells the judges he's done, and his time stops."

Three loops an' a dally. I was learning rodeo talk, and I soaked it up. I had the best explainer in the whole world—my daddy.

For weeks afterward I studied the rodeo program. Turk Greenough was there. He'd been raised in Red Lodge, Montana, and I was proud that a local rider was doing so well nationally. His very name had a cowboy ring to it: Turk Greenough.

Dad had ridden before he could walk. When he mounted Dan, his tall bay gelding, he did it quick and easy, then leaned over and placed his homemade right stirrup on the special-made boot for his bum leg. He looked so good sitting up on Dan, like he was part of the horse. His oldest brother, Jack, could sit a horse pretty, too, but when I was twelve it was my daddy who could do all things the best.

Rex and I had a dark brown, gentle mare we called Old Pet that I rode bareback around the corrals and nearby fields. Dad or a hired man would bridle her for me. To get on I led her alongside the corral poles or by a big rock and flopped on from there. Old Pet was patient, placid, and unflappable. She didn't mind my clumsy ways, and if I fell off she

Rex and me on Old Pet.

stood still and waited for me to gather myself up and lead her over to another rock. I never tried to get her out of a walk, but I was riding. Old Pet threaded her way through the trees in the outer corral, then plodded along in the three-cornered pasture while I dreamed:

The rodeo announcer intones, "Now, folks, here's Carole Flansburg, that great rodeo trick rider outta Clinton . . . Mon . . . tana." Carole. With an "e." Carole Lombard was my favorite movie star. I'd have to think of a prettier name than Flansburg though.

I had not yet learned to bridle Old Pet or get on without a rock to stand on or ride her over a walk when I began to wish for a "real" saddlehorse like the one the lady trick rider had. If I had one just like hers, I'd be just like her.

One day in the summer of 1942 my Uncle Jack drove up and led a bay mare down out of his horse trailer. He said her name was Pup. Dad had bought her from Charlie Lombard, his sister Zale's husband, as a surprise for me.

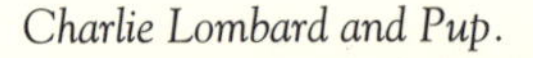

Charlie Lombard and Pup.

Jack led her across the highway over on the railroad right-of-way where he saddled and bridled her. I poked my left foot in the stirrup, heaved myself up, and kind of wallowed up the side of her. She side-stepped and shied at my clumsy efforts to clamber up into the saddle. This getting on wasn't as easy as it looked. Jack shouted, "Git up on there!" Before I had quite settled myself on my new perch, Jack whacked the halter across Pup's rump, and she took off like a jolting shot. I bounced from side to side, clawing to hang on. Back past Jack we came. He yelled, "Kick 'er into a run!" and waved his arms and swatted her with the halter again, giving Pup more momentum and me less aplomb. Jack must have thought he was doing me a favor, for every time we got close, he ran up and spooked her to run faster and shouted unintelligible instructions to me.

Somehow, some way, we got stopped and I got off. My legs had no bones in them; only my quivering flesh held me up. I thought, "This is no fun at all!" But I said what I knew I was expected to say: "Thanks, Jack. She's nice."

He handed me the halter and some more instructions that I heard in a daze, and he left.

I led Pup back across the highway. I tied her up to the corral with the bridle reins because I knew if I attempted the transfer of bridle to halter, I'd fumble around and lose her. I stood timidly patting her on the neck. I wanted to like her. I really did.

Pup was a gentle mare, but when she came in heat and saw other horses, she became a hard-mouthed little snot, and I was too inexperienced to hold her. She crow-hopped and danced sideways, and that scared me. I knew something was surely wrong with me because I should be happy. I'd got what I wanted, hadn't I? This whole thing wasn't as easy as the lady trick rider made it out to be. It seemed the trick was to stay on.

I pretended great joy and excitement when Dad came home from some errand and saw me with the new mare out at the barn.

Dad said, "You might as well learn to bridle 'er here as hereafter, don'tcha think?"

"Yeah," I answered, reluctant but game. Dad slipped her bridle off and looped the reins around her neck. I would really, really try to do just as he said.

"Now hold the bridle up to her head."

I did.

"Now say, 'Open your mouth.' "

I said, "Open your mouth."

Dad leaned on the corral gate, helpless with laughter.

He told that story on me many times, getting tickled again each time he told it. I'd give a sickly grin, trying to be a good sport about it and pretend it was as funny as Dad said it was.

I enjoyed forking hay into the workhorses' mangers from the window at their heads, but I wanted nothing to do with their heels. One time Dad sent me to the barn to get something over on the oat bin behind the cow stanchions. To get there I'd have to go behind four horse stalls. Chub and Molly never bothered me, but Dick and Duke, the two spooky blacks, always scared me. When I appeared at the barn door, they watched me with their heads in the air and their white eyes rolled backwards. I flinched; they flinched. I jumped; they jumped. Were they going to jump into their manger? Or jump backwards and kick me? I wished I could be like Dad and not be afraid of them. I was taking so long that he came over and ordered, "Speak to 'em an' walk on in!"

Serious and eager to do it right, I asked, "What'll I say?"

Dad dissolved in laughter. I was glad he wasn't mad at me.

That blaze-faced snaky Duke ran right over the top of me once. Dad ran him into the narrow arm of the corral so he could halter him, but Duke rolled the whites of his eyes and kept his hindquarters toward Dad and threatened to kick him. Dad yelled, "Turn around, you sonnuva *bitch*!" and commenced whacking him across the rump with the halter. Had I been Duke I wouldn't have wanted to turn around either. Duke decided his best route was over the top of the high fence, so Dad posted me outside the corral with a pole and said, "Every time he starts comin' over, paste 'im right between the horns."

"Now turn around!" he hollered. Whack! He larruped him across the rump again. Duke was less afraid of me than he was of Dad, so over the fence he came, with me hitting him lick after lick. He landed right on top of me and knocked me backwards. He stumbled over me, and in trying to gain his footing he rolled me over and over, bumping me along with his knees and feet. All I saw was black knees and white hooves and a big black underbelly on top of me. It all took place in slow motion, and I noticed for the first time that his underbelly hairs were not as black as the rest of him. After thirty feet of rolling he finally got untangled, and off he ran free as a bird.

Dad busted himself laughing about how funny I looked, but at the time I wasn't doing any laughing.

Dad teased me about the thorn brush. "How is it," he would ask in front of everyone, "how is it that I can dive off the trail into the thorn brush and chase out cows all the way up the draw and never get a scratch? An' you ride right up the main trail an' come home scratched all to hell? Never could figure that out."

Neither could I.

I turned myself wrong side out to do things "right" so Dad would admire my horsemanship, but there was never anything to admire. I couldn't cut the mustard. "You ride like a sacka beans," was my ultimate disgrace. Oh, why couldn't I be as unafraid as I was at two when he found me playing contentedly under some outlaw horse's belly? I was nothing at all what a Montana ranch girl should be.

It was August 3rd, my birthday. The cattle in the hills had sifted back down to the corrals at the Starvation Creek place. Dad tied salt blocks on Belle's packsaddle, swung up on Dan, and sang out to me, "Let's take 'em to the hills!" We pushed the cattle back up the draw to "The Saddle." The mountain we called Old Baldy rose up directly behind our home buildings and the Clinton Garage. As seen from the west, Old Baldy's top formed the pommel of a saddle; then it swaled down to the saddle seat, then rose higher to form the cantle. Coming from Missoula the mountain looked like a giant saddle. The lowest part of the seat was where we stopped to rest our horses.

I loved this view. Clinton lay below us, long and strung out over a mile. Tiny cars ran up Highway 10 headed for Missoula, Spokane, or Seattle. A freight train snailed its long uphill pull east toward Butte. A toy-size car stood waiting at the lower crossing; its occupants were probably counting the railroad cars as they click-thunked past.

Six years from then, in 1948, Dad would selectively log these hills. In ten years, 1952, Bonneville Power towers would march across the valley, and one tower would sit here in The Saddle with long spans of wires on either side. In the 1980s the cantle would be logged off in three ugly V's. But as we sat there on my thirteenth birthday on a summer day in 1942, none of these changes had yet taken place.

Lee Elliott took this picture on one of Dad's many elk-hunting trips into the South Fork of the Flathead River in the 1940s. This area is now called the Bob Marshall Wilderness. Left to right: Dad, Burl Flansburg, and Arnold Mueller.

We rode on toward Elliott's Cabin, a hunting cabin built by Lee Elliott's family in the early days. Here the grass was good. Dad unlashed the salt blocks, dropped them, and we rode on.

Dad got out a ways ahead of me and my horse, and I called, "Dad! Pup keeps wantin' to run and I don't want her to."

"Let 'er know who's boss," Dad answered and rode on out of sight. That was the problem: she knew who was boss, and it wasn't me. I rode way behind, muttering and fuming at Pup, for I had no idea how "letting her know who's boss" was done.

I heard a rifle shot. When I came in sight, Dad was cutting a little buck deer's throat. Without knowing it I had been along on a hunting trip as well as a salting trip. And it was out of season!

Dad quickly gutted him out and put the heart and liver in the saddlebags, then in answer to my questioning eyes said, "We're outta meat. This'll get us by till we can grain a dry cow. We'll come back tonight after dark and pack it out." At the first springs we came to, he washed the blood off his hands and skinning knife.

When we rode up to the yard we had company. My cousin Ebby and two of her friends were there. They jumped aboard Pup and galloped expertly around the garage. In the house I whispered, "Mom! There's a heart and liver in Pup's saddlebags!" She answered, "Just pay no attention." Finally, the company left.

Dad and I took Belle, the packhorse, and Pup and Dan, and left after dark for the hills again. The moon was a mere sliver. It was so very dark I wondered how Dad could ever find that place again, but these hills had been his back yard for the last thirty years. He soon had the deer tied on Belle, and we started back down.

I complained how rough riding Pup was once too often. Dad abruptly stopped, got off of Dan, and ordered, "Git up on my horse then!" More afraid of Dad than of his big horse, I crawled on and we came on home. What a surprise! Riding Dan was like sitting in a rocking chair even coming down off of steep places because he traveled with his back level at all times.

Dad told the story later:

"Lois was makin' so damn much noise I had to git way out in front of 'er or I'd never stand a chance of seein' a deer. I came up on this little buck sleepin' under a tree. He never got to his feet. Never knew what hit 'im. It oughta be pretty good meat. Comin' down offa the hill, Lois kept squallin' about Pup, so I told 'er ta git on Dan. . . . That Pup is a hard-ridin' little bitch."

Yes. Pup *was* a hard-ridin' little bitch, and it felt good to hear Dad admit it. I felt vindicated.

For more than half a lifetime I tried to feel like any western Montana girl "should" feel about horses. One day when I was fifty, I said aloud to myself, "I hate horses," and found that it was a great relief. I'm not the romantic, Old West, horsey kind of Montana ranch girl, but it's okay. I am still a Montana ranch girl. I have made peace with myself.

THE HAY DIGGERS, 1942

THE HAYING SMELLS of a western Montana July should be bottled. First mix up a combination of freshly mown alfalfa and wild hay cured in the hot sun, leather harness warmed by workhorses, prickly hay dust, and your own sweat. Then advertise it: "All of the nostalgia with none of the work." It would sell.

It's the summer of 1942. Haying season is in full swing on our ranch in the Clark Fork Valley east of Clinton. In the 1940s you can win bets it will rain twenty days in June, so we begin haying right after the 4th of July.

Dad mows with Dick and Duke, his "up an' comin'" team of black workhorses. It's a pretty sight to see them clatter round and around a green hayfield at a fast walk, laying it down. Dick and Duke are always Dad's team. They are nervous high steppers, and to put inexperienced or clumsy hands on their lines is to risk a runaway.

Dad and Rex watering the horses. Dad's favorite workhorse, Dick, is in the foreground.

"Dick'n Duke'r the best damn team I ever had on a mowin' machine," Dad declares. "You get a couple'a deadheads on a mower and they can't walk fast enough to keep the thicker hay from ballin' up. You're stoppin' and backin' up all the time to get untangled an' you can't get anything done." To not get anything done is the worst thing that can happen to Dad, for he has every year of the next thirty years planned, and he works that plan.

Except for a star on his forehead Dick is all black. He has a hammerheaded look, but his neck arches and his eyes and ears are alert. He's a high-spirited horse who meets his world assertively. Duke is the flightier of the two, but working in harness with Dick has a settling effect on him. They seem to say, "We're all business now."

I don't like either one of them myself. Ever since Duke jumped a fence and ran over the top of me, it soured me on him. Duke has a blaze face and four white feet. Dad says the Indians used to tell him:

"Four white feet and snow on his nose,

Sell him to the circus or feed him to the crows."

That's what I would have done with him.

In this wartime summer of '42 any man who is not 4F or too young or too old is in the service, which makes good help hard to find. Dad is thirty-eight and 4F because of his bum leg. He hires his older sister Olive to drive the rake team; she's as good a hand as many men half her age. Her team is Chub and Molly. Chub is a Belgian strawberry roan, and Molly is a solidly built dark sorrel mare that Dad raised from a colt out of Big Kneed Nell. Olive windrows the mown hay and then straddles the windrows and gathers it into bunches. The hay is now ready to stack.

Our neighbor Bob Covil and Dad trade work, and we put up all the hay on both places. Bob hooks a team to the overshot stacker and pulls it over to the highest spot on this field. A stack built here won't sit in a puddle and spoil. He stakes it down; then he hooks the team to the pull-up cable that raises the teeth loaded with hay up onto the stack. Meanwhile Dad and Dick and Duke on the buckrake are busy shoving a couple loads onto the spot where the stack will be. Bob crawls on top of it and begins to build the corners and sides of his stack. He makes the prettiest haystacks around, straight-sided, good corners, and topped off just so. Bob's stacks never leak or spoil or tumble down, and somehow he knows how big to form the base and when to begin topping it out so that when the stack is finished the field is empty.

The horse-drawn buckrake brings the loose hay to the stack. Pretend your left hand, palm up, is the buckrake. Your fingers are the teeth that scoop up the hay as the hand goes forward. Now picture a thumb on both sides of your left hand; these are Dick and Duke. Dad sits between them on the heel of your hand and guides the team so that the teeth straddle the shocks of bunched hay. Now loaded, they head for the stacker pushing their load of hay in front of them.

The fingers of your right hand, palm up, are the stacker teeth. Slide the buckrake teeth onto the stacker teeth. Back up; raise the buckrake teeth a bit with a foot lever, and poke the hay firmly onto the stacker so it doesn't fall off the front. Head back for another load. The overshot stacker sits at the end of the haystack with its teeth now full of hay.

Now my job begins. Babe and Belle, the stacker team, pull a cable out at right angles from the stacker, which raises the stacker arm and throws the hay up onto the haystack. The team backs up, lowering the stacker teeth to the ground.

Up on the stack Bob points to where he wants me to drop the load of hay. I take the lines, say "Get up" to Babe and Belle's gray and brown rumps, and drive out. They soon get smart and know just exactly how far they have to go before they reach the end. Oh, no! I've let them stop too soon. I feel stupid and sickened as I watch the whole load dribble down all over the stacker's arms and cables. Bob has to crawl down off the stack and dig the hay out of the stacker's insides, a slow, toilsome job. I help him, abject in humiliation. We pitch it one horse length away from the stack so Dad can pick it up later.

Dad is not happy with the delay. "Goddammit, I told you to keep that team a-goin'! Pound 'em on the tail if ya haf to!"

Determined not to let this happen again, I pound 'em on the tail the next load, but we're going too fast. Team and rigging recoil at the abrupt stop, and the load catapults clear over the stack. Shame and misery and extra work again, but this time the work is all mine. To everyone's surprise nothing is broken.

But the next time Bob stands leaning on his pitchfork with his tongue in his snoose lip and points, "Right there," I put it exactly there. I am in good graces again and my confidence seeps back. Most times I do it right, but it's those other times that I will remember.

Rex is the water boy. He's seven this year. When he was four and aboard his new Shetland pony for the first time, he observed, "I wish there was a 'teerin' wheel on this thing." By the time he will begin haying the war will be over, Dad will have retired the horses and mechanized the job, and Rex will shine.

Tip, our shepherd-collie dog, completes the hay crew. He smiles with his mouth open, chases gophers, dispatches water snakes, and is general manager of each phase of the operation.

Olive scatter-rakes, combing up every spear of dribbled hay. She drops one rake wheel into the foot-deep irrigation ditches to scrape doodles of hay away from ditch banks because a buckrake can break off a tooth on a ditch bank. Her right foot trips the teeth to dump the rake's load, and the left foot rests on a lever that holds the teeth firmly on the ground. From having driven the rake team last summer, I know it only takes once to learn to lift your left foot when you drop a wheel into the ditch, for it'll jolt your ankle and bring tears to your eyes if you forget. I see her stopped, bending over grimacing, and rubbing her left ankle.

A little before noon Dad calls out, "Let's button 'er up for dinner!"

We unhook our teams, exchange their bridles for halters, and lead them to water. They drink long from a quiet side pool of Starvation Creek. Skippers row themselves away to keep from being sucked up and swallowed. The animals lift their heads, and water drips off their soft velvet muzzles; they chew their water, then drop their heads and take another short drink. They stand tied, still in harness, lipping up their oats and slobbering with the goodness of it. We pile in the back of the old black pickup, barely tolerating Tip, who has rolled in nice fresh horse manure, and we go in for dinner.

On a ranch the noon and evening meals are called "dinner and supper," and they are equally big. Meat, spuds, gravy, a cooked vegetable, a salad, bread and butter, a dessert, coffee, lemonade, a toothpick, and some conversation. We listen to the noon news on the radio, and Dad has a roll-your-own. All his blue chambray shirt pockets bear the imprint of his can of Velvet tobacco.

After dinner Dad sings out, "Okay, all you hay diggers! Let's git out an' git 'er done!"

The stack grows. The field diminishes. Everyone clicks along in the rhythm of the job, and it feels good. Olive and her team, Chub and Molly, carefully scrape up and rebunch every doodle of hay, and when Olive nears the stack Rex takes the water jug over to her. Dick and Duke move purposefully around the field gathering up loads, coming into the stacker with proud, quick strides. All the horses' heads bob to move their shredded gunnysack nose-guards to shake off flies. Between pull-ups Babe and Belle bob their heads and kick horseflies off their bellies. Bob throws down a water snake that got tossed up with a load. I yelp and jump high and call Tip.

An Army convoy files by. I count the number of vehicles. Soldiers and sailors wave at us from troop trains on their way to those places on our wall maps. I wave back wishing I was older than thirteen. I'd like to have a sailor for a boyfriend like Pat and Ebby, Olive's eighteen-year-old twins. They are so pretty and are old enough for a boyfriend. I feel like I'll be just a kid forever.

I know from each day's news that the Germans are advancing in North Africa, and that fierce sea battles are raging in the South Pacific. How many of those soldiers and sailors hanging out the train windows grinning and waving will never come back? I know that I and my part of the world are being sheltered from war by those very servicemen on that troop train and others like them, and I am not too young or too unaware to be grateful for it.

The afternoon wears on. The sun feels hotter. No rain clouds in sight. No breakdowns. Just one load after another. When I see Bob beginning to top it off my interest revives, for we'll soon go home for supper.

The field's empty, the stack is topped out, and Bob rides down on the stacker teeth. The horses' gaits quicken, for they know it's quitting time too. When the horses are stripped of their harnesses they have a good roll in the corral dust. I count how many times each one makes a complete rollover. Some only make a half a roll, and one side doesn't get dusted. Dad says every time a horse makes a complete roll he's worth another hundred dollars. Dick is his favorite, and he's always worth the most. Chunky Chub is only worth fifty dollars today.

We ride back home. Bob always goes to his home for suppers. The rest of us troop into the houseful of good smells. Mom greets us from her hot kitchen. I peek under lidded pots and into big iron skillets that cover the black wood-burning cookstove. At the sink Mom is stemming a huge picking of her strawberries. I savor one the size and shape of a swallowtailed butterfly. Looks like we're having elk steak, mashed potatoes, milk gravy made from the steaks' skillet leavings, and fresh peas from the garden. A plate of green onions and red radishes are on the table. My saliva squirts and I take my turn at washing up, then take my place at the table.

Rex and I sit on the bench with the wall for our backrest. Thumbtacked above us are two maps, one for each side of the world, each theater of war. We get the news on the radio at every meal, and we follow our retreats and advances in the South Pacific and North Africa. Dad had bought a little cream-colored radio on Pearl Harbor Day thinking radios would be unavailable, and sure enough the next day when we declared war, no more radios were on the market. Someday when I am old, my grandchildren will call that little radio an "antique," and then I'll tell them about Edward R. Murrow and the "Lux Radio Theater" and the good music I used to get from Mexico and Calgary.

Supper is our social hour, and anybody who happens to stop in is invited to sit right down. Rube Boatman knocks at the door. Mom puts another plate on the big table as Dad asks, "Been t' supper? Sit down and rest yer hands and face."

After supper Dad rears back on the chair's two back legs and rolls a cigarette, a "pill," he calls it. He talks with a toothpick in the left side of his mouth and his cigarette in the right corner. "Well," he says, "we got that stack up and moved the stacker so we can hit it soon as the dew's off in the morning."

Moving a cabin in the Big Hole. There's a beaverslide stacker in the background.

Dad is checking the water in either his or Burl's Model T on their way to the Big Hole for haying season.

"Bob sure makes a pretty stack, doesn't he, Dad?" I say.

"Yep. Best in the valley." He flicks the ashes off onto his plate. He puts his roll-your-own back in his mouth, squints his right eye from the smoke, and recalls when he and his dad and brothers used to hay in the Big Hole each summer in the early '20s. Rex and I are tickled to hear his haying or logging or elk-hunting stories again even though we know most of them by heart.

"Loads went up the beaverslide so fast that the stacker just kept crawlin' on top of the load. He'd hit it a lick with his pitchfork at each end, and here'd come another one. There was three or four buckrakes bringin' in to one stack at a time, an' we really put up the hay. Those were well-built stacks, too. They call the Big Hole Basin 'The Land of the Ten Thousand Haystacks.'"

Talking about the Big Hole reminds him of mosquito stories.

"One time Burl an' I were goin' over to the Big Hole to go hayin'. We were drivin' Burl's ole Model T, an' it was a-heatin' up. So we stopped along a crick to get some water. The blood-hungry mosquitoes were so thick that Burl made three or four tries at the crick with a bucket an' finally came climbin' up the bank wavin' 'go on,' an' says 'The hell with it! Drive the sonuvabitch without water!' " We all laugh.

Rube Boatman says, "I hear mosquitoes are so big in Alaska that when one landed on an airstrip, they pumped fifty gallons of fuel into him before they realized it wasn't a P38." And we all laugh some more.

Dessert time brings the big blue enamel mixing bowl full of strawberries. We scoop them into large mush bowls and add Creamy's cream. Sugar is added sparingly, for it takes ration stamps. So-o good! More conversation and jokes and stories.

Finally Mom and Olive and I clear the table and wash the dishes and reset the table for breakfast to get a jump on the early morning chores. We lug the quarts of green beans that Mom canned today down into the root cellar.

Dad limps out to the garage to work on a neighbor's car and sharpen sickles so they'll be ready for the next mowing.

Rex refills Mom's empty woodbox, then ambles out to the barn with the milk bucket to milk Creamy.

Rube Boatman is our irrigator. He fits a cigarette into his cigarette holder with fingers that had once been haggled by a buzz saw, shoulders his shovel, and strolls out to the three-cornered pasture whistling his continual tuneless tune through his front teeth. Somehow Rube can place his canvas dams in ditches so as to make water run uphill. He instructed me once, "Irrigate the high spots. The low ones can take care of themselves."

And so the summer goes. When the last stack of the season is up, Dad buys a case of beer for the men and a case of pop for the women and kids. He pays me twenty dollars for the summer's haying job and says I did a good job. Money is not as tight as it was in the Depression, before the war started. My twenty dollars all in one chunk feels good. I feel pride in my honest money that came from honest work. My stacker flub-ups are behind me.

I tell Mom, "Dad says I did a good job!"

LIFE AT DIXON, 1930S

IN 1930 DAD'S SISTER OLIVE went to work as head cook at the Northern Pacific Hospital in Missoula (where Providence Center now stands), and because she had only one small room at the hospital as her quarters, she took her four children, ages four to nine, to live with Gramma and Grampa Flansburg at Dixon. The kids missed their mother, but life at Dixon was good.

Little four-year-old Cal adored Grampa, and when Grampa called him "my bully boy" it made him feel he was someone very special. He wanted to be just like Grampa, down to the shaved head. Grampa obliged and shaved Cal's head, too, but only once—Cal didn't like his looks. Pat and Ebby thought it an honor when Grampa asked one of them to clipper off his grizzled hair.

Grampa kept Santa Claus and the Easter Bunny alive for his little Smith grandkids by making large footprints in the snow under the chimney on Christmas Eve and by throwing Easter-egg dye out by the fence. There it was. Solid proof they had been there.

A movie at the Dixon theater was ten cents, and a new one came every week. The kids hit Grampa up for enough to see a show, and he'd say, "Go put the touch on Alice an' see how you come out." Gramma would get her purse, then fish her little change purse out of it. Then she would either turn her back on them or go in the bedroom so they couldn't see in her purse, and come up with a few cents for each of them. They'd go to Grampa, and he'd make up the difference so they could see a show. After one movie they told Grampa the story of Tyrone Power in *Jesse James*. Grampa said, "Well they sure as hell didn't get that right, did they? I lived neighbors to 'im in Missouri, an' he was one mean son of a bitch." He added that Frank James once sold him a pair of shoes when Frank was working as a shoe clerk in Minnesota.

On one day of every fall Grampa flagged down the train at Dixon and went to Missoula to the M.M. to order the winter groceries. That same evening he came back saying, "The order'll be here tomorrow."

Olive's children when they went to live with Gramma and Grampa at Dixon: Ode is nine, twins Pat and Ebby are six, and Cal is four. Ode's twin sister, Doll, died at two.

What fun it was to ride in the wagon down to the depot the next day! The train stopped and set their stuff out on the railroad platform. There were several one-hundred-pound sacks of flour and sugar, some cases of canned milk, a keg of apple cider, two or three large bricks of cheese, big boxes of raisins, and bulk sacks of oatmeal. Spaghetti came in a box a foot wide, a foot deep, and four feet long. Coffee was in a big tall red-and-gold bucket with a side view of a turbaned Turk in a long white robe, walking along, arms up, holding a cup of coffee to his lips with both hands.

Grampa loaded it all on the wagon, the kids piled on, and Ned and Brady pulled them back up the hill and down the bench road to the house. The year's groceries were stored in the basement. In that basement were kegs of lard, a crock of eggs preserved in water glass (a colorless syrupy solution of either sodium or potassium silicate), and hams that Grampa had cured with big yellow cans of Morton's salt. They butchered a fat hog in the fall, for Grampa liked his bacon fat and greasy and salty. He was of the mind that if a little was good a lot was better, so he pumped more than enough Morton's salt into the meat to cure it, so much that Gramma parboiled it before frying.

Jars and jars of Gramma's canned garden vegetables and fruits lined the shelves, as did large cans of spices, pudding mixes, and quarts of vanilla extract she bought from the Watkins man—the itinerant peddler of such stuff plus household remedies and bag balm for cows. The kids don't ever remember being served the pudding mixes, and there

Gramma Flansburg holding Burley, Burl's oldest child.

were bottles of almond extract that Gramma never used, but every time the Watkins man came Gramma bought something. She never went anywhere or visited her neighbor ladies unless they came to her house, so she must have been lonely for adult company and probably thought if she bought something, he'd stay longer. She never embraced any particular religion, but she welcomed the Jehovah's Witnesses. They would stay and visit with her hour after hour.

No doubt loneliness was one of the reasons Gramma never could turn down a salesman. After Grampa died she once bought an electric vacuum cleaner. But she had no electricity. Olive took it back to the salesman and scolded him for taking advantage of Gramma. When Gramma was sixty-eight a salesman sold her a twenty-five-year subscription to *The Farm Journal.* He probably left chuckling, but she was only two years shy of outliving it.

Dad thought that with four kids to raise, a cow would be a good thing for Gramma and Grampa to have, so he gave them a Guernsey to milk. Grampa could milk fast but didn't do it very often. Gramma usually did the milking, first with one hand until it got tired, then with the other—squirt . . . squirt . . . squirt.

Refrigeration at the time was a cloth-covered box on the dirt floor of the basement and was just a little bit better than nothing. Gramma set shallow pans of milk around the house. When the cream rose, she scooped it off and used it for coffee till it soured, then baked with it. The milk she let sour and made cottage cheese.

But nobody really liked the cow, or bringing her in from the hills at milking time, or milking her, or drinking warm milk. So the cow just sort of hung around until she died. Gramma and Grampa's lifestyle in logging camps hadn't included a cow, and even though they were settled now, they preferred horses and Morning Milk canned milk. Though it wasn't original, Ollie thought this fit them:

"Morning Milk's the best of all,
Comes in cans both large and small.
No tits to pull, no shit to pitch,
Just punch a hole in the son of a bitch."

Whenever the kids saw Grampa come by with his teams and a wagonload of logs, they ran out along the road. He stopped and lifted each child up on the load, and they rode with him to the railroad siding

Grampa and "four up" perched on a one-log load in McDonald Basin north of Dixon, 1916.

in Dixon; there they watched him load the logs onto the flatcars that went to Bonner Mill.

Cal remembers seeing Grampa way down the road coming home at the end of a day with "four or six up." From as far away as he could see them he knew it was Grampa because his gray horse called Rock stood out among the bays and browns and blacks.

Cal, the youngest of the four, tells it:

"All us kids would run to meet him, and Grampa set each of us up on one of his horses, and we'd ride home. He always put me up on Rock. Nobody else ever got to ride Rock. Just me. At the barn Grampa would unhook the tugs, and while the horses were still harnessed and us still ridin' 'em, they'd go up to the ditch to get a drink. Rock would take his long drink, raise his head up and slobber a little bit, then take another drink, and go back to the barn. As soon as Grampa took his harness off, Rock'd shake himself all over. The other kids' horses never waited to get their harnesses off before they shook. They'd take a drink and start shakin', and the kids'd hang on for Chris'sake tryin' to stay on. . . . Did you ever try to stay on a horse when he's shakin'?"

All four soon learned to be expert riders.

Grampa's old gray, Mike, could outrun any horse in the county in a kids' impromptu horse race. Pat thought Grampa was so wise because when it came to horses he could practically tell the future. Once when she was in the eighth grade, she saddled Mike to go down to Dixon to watch a baseball game. Grampa said, "A foul ball'll hit Mike in the head, an' he'll buck you off." She sat on Mike near home plate with one leg cocked over the saddle horn, posing prettily (for boys were looking) when that very thing happened. "How'd he know?" she thought.

Grampa made his living with his horses. After the family moved from Clinton to Dixon he logged around Dixon, McDonald, and Evaro. He freighted for the Teddy mine for a time until a road good enough for trucks was built. He loaded logs on log cars at the Dixon railroad siding, subcontracted for Buck Helean on road construction jobs, put up hay, got in firewood, and did some horseshoeing for people.

When it came to using the principles of leverage, Grampa was an artist. An old tall metal smokestack with bricks around it stood at the east end of Dixon. Its bricks were falling off, a fascination that drew the town's kids to play there. Dixon's city fathers approached Grampa to take the unsafe smokestack down.

He gathered up his cables and blocks, took two or three horses, and spent two days stringing out and hooking up his rigging. Some folks complained. "Two whole days, and nothing's done!" they said to each other.

When all was ready, he spoke to his teams, "Inch," and they moved an inch. "Inch," he repeated, and they moved another inch and carefully tightened the tugs. When he said "Take 'er away!" the smokestack slowly lowered and lay over so gently it didn't even bend.

One of Grampa's jobs was keeping the Dixon bridge free of debris for Sanders County. He kept a close eye on that old bridge. In high-water time, in addition to his own trips to the bridge, he taught his grandkids what to look for and sent one of them down two or three times a day to check out the bridge. He questioned them: Was the tree on a pier? Or on the piling? How long was it? He loaded his wagon with cables and blocks, gathered up his long pike pole with a hook on it, and threw on a swamp hook he'd made from a latch off an old peavy (canthook).

If school was out the grandkids got to go ride along in the wagon to the bridge and listen to Grampa recite "The Cremation of Sam Magee" and other long poems. Or he sang old songs with lots of verses like "The Arkansas Traveler" or the one that said at the end of every verse, "Plant yer taters in the sandy land!"

He drove his team and wagon down the hill and past the schoolhouse. If school was in session, one of the pupils threw open a window so they could all hear Old Man Flansburg come by affectionately cussing his horses. The story also goes that the teacher closed the window when she heard him coming. Both accounts are accurate.

At the Dixon bridge Grampa looked the situation over. This particular time that Cal tells about, a cottonwood tree was jammed nearly the full length of the bridge; the high muddy river boiled against it, and the old bridge shuddered and rocked from the strain of it all. With his pike pole Grampa hooked his blocks and tackles, cables and pulleys to the tree and the bridge from angles that used the forces of gravity and the river's current in his favor. Everything had to be set up for this to turn loose, that to turn loose, then all to release without taking his rigging downriver along with the tree. When all was ready, Grampa picked up the lines and said, "Inch." Ned and Pat moved an inch to tighten the tugs; then, "Take 'er away, Ned!"

Cal watched what happened next with awe and amazement and pride in Grampa's ability. As if manipulated by giant invisible fingers, that great, long, leafy cottonwood backed up the river against the current just far enough to clear; then it slowly turned forty-five degrees until it pointed down the river, floated straight on through under the bridge, and bobbed its way west on down the Flathead River.

Grampa picked up his rigging and went home.

GRAMMA'S WASHING MACHINE, 1935

OLIVE GOT A HALF DAY OFF every week and one full day off every two weeks. About once a month she used her NP Railroad pass to visit her kids and help her parents.

She arrived at Dixon at 12:30 in the afternoon and had to catch the train back to Missoula at 4:30 the next morning in time to cook the hospital breakfast. The train didn't stop at Dixon unless you flagged it. She would be at the depot a little before 4:30 A.M. while it was still dark out. She'd hear the train coming way off yonder, and when it came in sight she'd step onto the track and begin to wave a rag or a shirt, something big enough to catch the engineer's attention. He'd give two short bursts on his whistle to let her know he had seen her and stop and pick her up.

Olive's two boys were four-year-old Calvin and nine-year-old Olin, named after Grampa—we called him Ode (pronounced O-dee). Ode's twin sister, Doll, died when she was two years old. The six-year-old twin girls, Elinor and Evlyn, were called Pat and Ebby. True to form, Grampa had his own pet names for the four of them: Blister, Cocky, Peg, and Midget.

That first little rented house on top of the bench behind Dixon somehow held seven people in its tiny front room, kitchen, and two wee bedrooms. A path led to the outhouse out back. When Dutch, the last of Gramma and Grampa's kids, graduated from Dixon High School in 1930, and when Ode and Cal got big enough to sleep out in "the big shed," things became somewhat less crowded.

That "big shed" out back of the house had a lean-to on it they called "the little shed." Here Gramma did the washing, first on a washboard, and later in an old wooden tub on three legs. The washtub had a handle on one side, and in its lid were imbedded several sticks four inches long. When you closed the lid and pushed the handle back and forth, the sticks went up and down and around at the same time and agitated

Left to right: Dutch, Zale, and Gramma at the first old house at Dixon, where Gramma got her "brand-new" secondhand washing machine.

the clothes. Cranking the tub handle was easy enough for one of the kids to do, but the hand-cranked wringer didn't turn easily, and no little kid could do it. Gramma did that herself. Gramma's wash day was often when Olive came up.

During the week, the family put their dirty clothes in "the dirty clothes bag" in the little shed. When it got full, they just pitched them in on top of the heap until it became "the dirty clothes pile." Clothes had to be really dirty or smelly before anyone changed them—not just worn one day as we do in these days of automatic washers and dryers. Even so, with seven people tossing their dirties onto the pile, the washing soon grew big and ugly.

Gramma hated washing clothes.

Early one summer morning a Maytag salesman came to the door. Gramma invited him in and quickly agreed to let him give her a demonstration with his demo machine. The man jockeyed it out of the back seat of his new Plymouth saying, "We'll just set this up in your house and . . . you don't do laundry in your house?"

Gramma detoured him to the little shed. He set the machine alongside the towering dirty clothes pile.

"Now," he says, "Where's your water faucets?"

He was dismayed to learn that you got the water from the big irrigation ditch several hundred yards up the hill above the house.

"Oh! . . . How do you get it here?"

In a barrel. With a horse hitched to a stoneboat.

"Do you drink that water, too?"

Oh, sure.

The salesman made a mental note not to take a drink at this house. He was puzzled. "How're we gonna get wash water here when your husband isn't here to drive the horse?"

Well, she suggested, the salesman could pull the stoneboat with *his* car if he wanted to.

He was game. He and the grandkids buzzed up the hill to the irrigation ditch. The ditch water had traveled through Rickert's sheep farm. As they all bailed the yellow water into the barrel, he inquired of the kids, "Do you really drink this water, too?"

The kids said yes. Except when the ditch gets too low to dip out of and gets to be only a muddy puddle.

"What d'ya do then?"

Well, then Grampa gets it out of the Jocko River.

"How's he do that?"

He drives the team and wagon right into the river just below that place where the Indians hold their stick games—you know that place?—and he fills the barrel there.

"Doesn't anybody get sick?"

Nope.

The salesman had to admit that these four little kids and their grandmother sure looked and acted healthy and vigorous. He dragged the stoneboat back to the little shed behind his new Plymouth. "This machine washes better in hot water," he said.

To get hot water, Gramma told him, you get the fire going in the shed stove, which she had done while he was getting the water, and you heat it up in a boiler.

"A-a-all right."

About noon the water was ready and dumped into the washing machine. The salesman tromped on the pedal and started the Maytag's gas motor.

As Gramma happily gave the proceedings her full attention, the salesman washed on that pile of clothes. And he washed. And washed. Gramma was impressed.

Sensing victory and a sale, he rattled on, "You can wash anything with this machine—pillows, blankets—anything!"

Gramma had him wash their pillows, then their blankets. Toward evening she sent the kids out to the barn to get the saddle blankets. And after dark that poor son of a bitch was still washing.

"This machine, as you can see, can wash anything, Mrs. Flansburg. A new one just like this demonstrator is only one hundred thirty-nine dollars."

Gramma said she'd take it.

Grampa came home for supper and said, "No."

"We also have a used machine I'll sell you for eighty-five dollars, Mr. Flansburg, and I'll give you five dollars for your old one."

Grampa said okay, and Gramma had a new washing machine.

That salesman earned his commission. What's more, he did it without taking a drink of water all day.

For a while they really liked the new washing machine. Its gas motor went "Putt putt . . . putt . . . putt putt putt . . . putt . . . putt." But Gramma and Grampa weren't raised in the age of motors and engines, and when after a time the motor grew notional and wouldn't go, wash days perplexed them. The machine would start off as nice as you please and then stop. While Gramma and Grampa wondered why it stopped, and stood and looked at it, and Grampa cussed it, the water got cold. Gramma dipped the water back into the boiler and reheated it, then bailed it back into the washing machine. She stomped on the pedal and . . . no go.

"Go get Carmen," Grampa ordered, and one of the kids biked or rode a horse down the hill for Carmen Ebel, Dixon's garageman. Carmen started the machine. As soon as he left, it wouldn't start again.

Once during mealtime they heard it run out of gas and quit. Grampa told Cal, "Blister, go out and shut it off so it won't run down the battery."

Cal, who was now eight or ten and old enough to have learned such things, answered, "It doesn't run on a battery, Grampa."

"I *said*, go out and shut it off so it doesn't run the battery down!"

Cal went out and dutifully pushed a little piece of metal over onto a pin. It was useless to try to convince Grampa there was no battery anywhere on it.

When Cal was fourteen he made some money on a sheep shearing job, and he bought a little motor to mount on his bicycle. Some time later he hooked that motor to Gramma's washer. It really washed clothes. In fact it ran so fast the washer danced on the floor. The motor ran backwards which didn't alter the washer's performance, but it made the wringer spit the clothes backwards so it refused to take them into its rollers. Cal turned the wringer around and put the clothes into it the other way, and it fairly slurped them up. It was a going concern, but Gramma was afraid of it. Olive did the washings after that on her day off.

Cal now lives in Gramma and Grampa's old house where he was raised.

"Where is that old Maytag now?" I asked him.

"Still sittin' out here in the yard."

We went out to take a look at it. There, hunkered down under the lilac bush, a few handy steps from the clothesline sat Gramma's old secondhand washing machine. The old girl graciously received us and accepted our compliments.

"I see its black-and-white wringer rollers are as good as new," I say.

"Yep, she's a little weather-worn, but she still works," Cal says. "Mary washed with it out here last summer."

"Washed clothes real well, too," says Mary, Cal's wife.

Cal's reply: "Always did. What buffaloed Gramma an' Grampa was that little bitty gas motor."

GRAMPA'S WAY

MARK TWAIN SAID, "I have never let my schooling interfere with my education." Neither did Grampa. He told the census taker he had been to the fourth grade, "but I can add a column of figures as long as your arm and have the answer before you can say it."

Like Dad, Grampa read slowly but retained what he read with a near-photographic memory. He subscribed to and read from cover to cover the *Saturday Evening Post*, *Forbes*, *Time*, *Business*, the *Literary Digest*, and both the morning and evening Spokane newspapers; and he discussed their contents with anyone who wanted to talk. He and Dad had great fun talking politics. Both were staunch Republicans and FDR bashers. They agreed that FDR "didn't know if Christ was crucified or hooked to death by a blind cow."

In his bookcase were some of O. Henry's works, all of Kipling's, and most of Mark Twain's, his favorite and often quoted author. There was a complete set of encyclopedias. Grampa knew how to find what he wanted to know in the tissue-paper-thin pages, but nobody else ever used them.

He read clenching his short-stemmed pipe between his teeth, spitting occasionally into the heater's pan of ashes that sat conveniently between his feet. I watched him once reading, puffing, and spitting. Snow melted off his boots and ran in a puddle around the ash pan. He noticed it, misdiagnosed the problem, and said to himself in a surprised and injured tone, "Well, the goddamn thing leaks."

Logging was in Grampa's blood and was his favorite thing. The last time he logged he broke his pelvis. That winter he and his neighbor, Ken Browning, were getting out some logs on the hill behind his place. They brought the logs down on a dray, which was like the front axles of a bobsled without the back. One end of the logs rode on the dray, and the back end of the logs dragged behind in the snow. Grampa rode up on the dray sitting on a "dry ass," a gunnysack filled with hay.

Ken opened a wire gate, and as the team pulled on through, the dray runner hit a rock; the sudden jerk threw Grampa off his perch down underneath the dragging logs. He hollered "Whoa!" but the team couldn't stop with the logs pushing them downhill in the snow. The log ends tossed and tumbled Grampa under them and then dragged over top of him. Ken got the team stopped and looked back to see Grampa crawling up from under the logs saying, "Kenneth, I'm all broke to hell."

Ken was resourceful and could have rigged up a travois or some such thing to get Grampa down out of the hills, but Grampa insisted that Ken help him get up onto Old Riley. With a fractured pelvis he rode down out of the hills on that rawboned horse.

Cal thought it odd that Grampa was not stopping at the barn, but rode up to the house instead. Grampa said, "Well, goddamn it, don't stand there lookin' at me like a graven image! Help me down offa this horse!" Cal got him into the house and into bed. He refused to go to a doctor or have one come to the house. He was delirious for two days, and neither Cal nor Gramma could do anything with him.

Finally Cal asked one of his high school teachers to help him get Grampa to the NP Hospital in Missoula. Once there, he refused to take off his long-handled wool underwear. He wouldn't take a shot or do anything else the doctor and nurses wanted him to do.

"Get Sal up here! She's runnin' this place anyway," he ordered.

So Olive, the head cook, was called up from the kitchen, but she couldn't do anything with him either. Within a week the doctor said, "You may as well take him home. We can't do anything with him here."

An ambulance took him home. As they drove slowly through Dixon the driver turned on the siren, and Grampa stuck his head up to see how many people were watching him come into town. At the house he refused to allow the ambulance attendants to help him inside. "Blister c'n do it." So Blister did.

When Ken Browning came over to visit, Grampa told 'em tall and scary about his hospital experience. "Kenneth," he says, "I had one helluva time in that hospital."

From the other side of the room Olive added, "We did, too."

Within a few weeks he was up and about and out at the barn talking to his horses again. Every day he gave each of them some oats and sat out in the barn or corral petting and talking to each one. He often said, "My horses've pulled every time I asked 'em to. They don't owe me a thing."

After he broke his pelvis, he turned his horses out to eat on the haystacks. Even if they ate the bottom of the stack out first and it fell over on them, and Cal had to hitch up a team and pull them out from under it, that didn't bother Grampa. He said, "They put up that hay; they c'n eat it."

Grampa liked things done "right," which meant the way he'd always done it. Dad built a power buckrake and sent it up to put up Grampa's hay. After Grampa stood awhile leaning on a fencepost, chin on his arms, watching Jake run around the field gathering up hay quickly and efficiently, he told Jake to get the thing off his place, that it wasn't "right," and that he would put it up with his horses. Which he did.

One time Ode rigged up Grampa's drag saw so it would cut blocks of wood off faster, but Grampa said it wasn't "right," and told him to fix it back the way it was.

The "right" way to haul water was with a horse hooked to a stoneboat. One time Dad and Rex were at Dixon with a flatbed truck. Dad said to Rex, who was eight and had learned how to drive the truck, "Well, go get the truck an' we'll go up an' get some water."

Delighted to show off his driving ability, Rex bounced over and started it up. Grampa sat down on the bumper. Rex sang out, "You'll have to move, Grampa. We're gonna go get some water for ya!"

Grampa didn't move or even look around, but muttered, "Ain't no goddamn kid gonna back over every damn thing I got around here."

Rex told Dad, and Dad grinned and said, "Well, I guess we won't haul water today."

Dad says when he was growing up, for some reason he could never figure out, Grampa would drive right on past a spring and make camp somewhere—anywhere—where they'd have to haul water to camp.

One time the old gray horse he called Rock got over the fence onto Strombo's place and fell through their root cellar. They got him out, but he was so hurt and stoved up that he'd never be any good again. Grampa didn't want to shoot him or have anyone else do it either, so when the man at the fish hatchery in Arlee offered him two dollars for him, Grampa took it. The fish hatchery man came down and loaded him up and trucked him the sixteen miles to Arlee. Two days later Rock found his way back home. Here came the fish hatchery man to get his fish food back. Grampa said, "No. Rock's come home to die," and he refunded the man his two dollars.

Dad suggested Grampa consider letting him truck ten or fifteen of his older horses to the cannery in Butte. "They're eatin' you outa house an' home, Dad, and you might get a little somethin' out of 'em."

Grampa thought that was a good idea, and he began to tick off on his fingers which ones he'd sell. "Le'see. There's Kate. . . . She's an able old bitch; I'll keep her. There's ole Brady. . . . He's got that bad foot. But I c'n fix that. . . ."

There was a little bit wrong with this one and that one, "but I c'n fix that." He finally got down to one and told Gramma he was going to send old Lucy to the cannery.

"No," she said. "She's the only one that'll eat out of my hand over the garden fence."

So Grampa told Dad, "They've lived all their life here, an' they're gonna die here."

Like his horses, Grampa eventually died there, too.

All during World War II Grampa said he wanted to live until the boys came home.

In 1917 his boys, Jack and Burl, were drafted into the Army. Jack spent his stretch logging for the Army in the Northwest around Oregon, while Burl was based around San Francisco and put in his Army time prizefighting. He was the Army's undefeated champion of the West Coast. When they were mustered out at the war's end, they both returned to Clinton and resumed logging with Grampa, Jim, and Jake.

On December 7th, 1941, Burl's stepson, Joe Marling, became the first Montana serviceman lost in World War II; he was killed when the battleship *Arizona* was bombed and sunk in Pearl Harbor. Four more of Grampa's grandsons joined the service. Each night before he went to bed, he stood before their photos on the piano, and touched their faces, and murmured, "Well, little buckos, I hope you make it through another day."

When the war ended in August of 1945, another generation of Grampa's boys came home. All but little Joe Marling.

Ken Browning was fencing up on the hill back of the place late in July of 1946. Visiting with his friend, Grampa remarked, "Kenneth, I'm satisfied with the life I've lived."

On July 26th, a Friday, Grampa got out his grip of shaving stuff from where he kept it under his bed and began to shave. The small low mirror in the kitchen was just the right height for Gramma to see herself; and as was his habit, instead of hanging the mirror on a higher nail on the wall for him to see well, he spraddled his legs out and bent to his business of shaving. He shaved only on Sundays.

"Olin, why are you shaving today? It's not Sunday," Gramma asked.

"Because I'm gonna kick the bucket today, an' I don't want all these whiskers on in my coffin. Tell Kenneth to stick around today."

Gramma paid no attention, but went out to chase a chicken out of the garden. She heard a thump. She ran in and found Grampa dead on the floor. He had taken the last swipe at the last whisker, put his straight razor in his shirt pocket, and still had shaving soap on his face.

Gramma ran up the hill and got Ken. He ran to the house, then went to Dixon to phone the undertaker.

Grampa had been having a few chest pains but chose not to see a doctor. He died of a heart attack at seventy-seven.

GRAMMA DIES, 1961

AFTER GRAMPA FLANSBURG DIED, Gramma lived fourteen more years and died at ninety-one on April 2nd, 1961.

For a few weeks after Grampa died, Olive stayed with Gramma; then whichever child or grandchild who was most free stayed with her so she'd not be alone. Cal and Ode even hired some old guy to stay there with her for a time when no one else was able to.

For about fifteen years, from the late '20s to the early '40s, the Big Ditch and the Jocko River had been Gramma and Grampa's only sources of water. Cal says, "Water was H_2O and whatever else happened to be in it." Before Ode went into the Army in 1942, he developed a spring up on the hill above the house. He dug it out, boxed it in, and piped it fifty or sixty feet across the irrigation ditch. They had good spring water after that, but they still had to haul it until two or three years after Grampa died. In '48 or '49 Burl dug the water line, Olive bought the pipe, and Bob Lantz of Dixon plumbed the spring water into the house.

But Gramma still saved water. Not only did she use laundry wash water until it was black and unable to clean anything, she washed dishes in the least water possible. She drew about two inches of water from the new tap into her gray enamel dishpan. She saved soap like she saved water. She gave a bar of Fels Naphtha a couple of turns between her hands in the dishpan, enough to say she had soap, but not enough to make a sud. She washed the meal's dishes. Her dishwater became crowded with gunk, and a quarter inch of grease floated on top. She flicked her fingers on top of the water to chase a spot clear of grease, plunged in a plate or cup, and washed it. The whole pile of dishes got the same water, for to change water was to waste water.

She visited us at Clinton once when I was eight or nine. While I dried she "washed" our dishes in her two inches of thick dishwater. I rinsed them real good with hot water from the teakettle and ventured, "Gramma, we have lots of water." She mumbled something I didn't catch, but I gathered she'd been doing this job all her life and knew how it was done and didn't care to be corrected by some kid.

After a time Ode moved in with Gramma because he thought he might like to farm the eighty-acre place.

Once, Ode loaned one of Grampa's horses to a neighbor. Gramma said nothing, but after brooding about it for a week, she said, "Bring my horse back." It had never occurred to Ode to ask Gramma about the transaction, for he had grown up seeing Grampa and the males of the family calling all the shots and making all the decisions. With Grampa gone, it was her horse. Gramma got a heady taste of ownership, and it became "*my* paper, *my* magazine, *my* hay." Ode couldn't take her pendulum swing from complete passivity to possessive assertiveness, and he soon gave up the idea of farming *her* place.

But before he left he took Gramma on a trip back to Oklahoma to see her sisters, Artie and Rosa, whom she hadn't seen since she boarded the Immigration Train at Kansas City for Calgary nearly fifty years before.

The last two or three years of her life Gramma's mind began to fail. She thought she heard babies crying and would say, "Pick up that baby!"

Gramma's funeral was the last time all nine of her children were together; none are living now. Back row, left to right: Zale, Olive, Midge, Ollie, Dutch; front row, left to right: Jack, Jake, Burl, Jim.

She misidentified people and called Pat, her granddaughter, "Rosie" (Gramma's little sister).

Dad's sister Dutch took Gramma for awhile to her home in Missoula until one night, unknown to the sleeping family, Gramma slipped out. The police found her wandering about the dark streets, barefoot, in her flannel nightgown, and they called Dutch. All Gramma knew was that she was "at Dulce's." It must have taken a bit of sleuthing to find out who to call.

Olive took her back to Dixon.

One day Gramma complained of severe belly pain. Olive took her to the doctor who put her in the hospital in St. Ignatius. Olive called Ollie in Jackson, Montana, and Ollie drove up immediately. The doctor told the twins that Gramma had a bowel obstruction, and although surgery was indicated, the odds were that she might not survive the

All but five of Grampa and Gramma's fourteen grandchildren were at her funeral. Back row, left to right: Cal Smith, Ode Smith, Rex Flansburg, Kenneth Krause (Ollie's son), and Burley Flansburg; front row, left to right: Susie Flansburg Maez and Olive Flansburg Smollack (Burl's girls), Elinor (Pat) Smith Kind, Evlyn (Ebby) Smith Larson, and Lois Flansburg Hedgers. The five who couldn't be there were: Hazel Jean Flansburg Poland (Burl's eldest girl), Bob and Judy Flansburg (Jake's children), and Dulce Matt Burland and Verna Matt Combs (Midge's girls).

operation because of her general debility and frailty and advanced age. Faced with the fact that either way both suffering and death were imminent, Olive and Ollie agonized over the wrenching no-win decision. They decided not to put her through the additional pain of surgery, and they stayed with her the next several hours holding her hand, talking to her, and seeing to it she was given the hypos as often as possible. Gramma's last words were: "Don't let me die." A few minutes later Gramma drew in her last breath, and she was gone. The twins wept and watched the lines of agony and worry flow out of her features like water seeking its own level, leaving a smooth peace on the face of the little shell of what was once their mother.

The day before Gramma's funeral Olive and Ollie went to see her "lying in state."

"Something's wrong. . . . What is it?"

"I don't know. . . . What is it?"

"The black band is missing."

"That's it."

They informed the funeral director who said he had not known what that little black velvet band in her bundle of clothes was for. He fastened it around her neck.

"There," they said, "That's Mama."

At the funeral we all gathered around to see her for the last time. She lay in her coffin, dressed in her navy blue best dress with the little black velvet band around her throat. But there was still something missing . . . she was so very still. . . .

The button. Gramma was no longer chewing on her button.

She was really gone.

THE BIG TREE, 1947

WHENEVER I FELT the need for solitude, I climbed Old Baldy behind our house to sit at the foot of my Big Tree. From beneath its lofty branches my eyes caressed the panorama of our narrow mountain valley below me while I reflected on Life.

One late afternoon I got off the high school bus and looked up at Old Baldy behind our place. My Big Tree was gone! A yellowish stump and a wide scruffy swath in the snow below it gave mute evidence of its fate.

That ponderous old yellow pine had taken off like a bullet, they said, plunged down the hillside, jumped the Big Ditch, plowed out over the three-cornered pasture and through the fence, and came to a stop about fifty feet from the highway.

It was the winter of 1947. Dad needed a machine shed, and he decided to use the trees on Old Baldy for the lumber to build one. He knew he wasn't able to fall the trees because with his stiff-kneed bum leg he was no longer catty enough to get out of the way if a tree split and barber-chaired or started off the stump the wrong direction. So he hired Cal Smith, my twenty-two-year-old cousin, and Bill Pond as fallers.

When they dropped the trees with their crosscut saw, the tree-lengths shot off the snow-covered mountain to the bottom. After the falling was finished, those trees that hadn't run to the bottom had to be hand logged—that is, turned or rolled or pried loose from brush and helped to the bottom of the hill. With Cal to help him, Dad took on this job because he was good with a canthook and didn't have to be as fast on his feet.

To get down off the snowy hillside in a hurry at the end of a day, Dad held his stiff bum leg straight out in front of him and skied down on his rubber-booted good left foot. Down he flew over the bumps and terraces left on the hillside when Glacial Lake Missoula receded a couple of million years ago.

Late one afternoon while he was sailing downhill on his good foot (long enough to be a ski), the bum foot caught on something and stuck in the ground; over he went, ass over teakettle, and cartwheeled down the mountain. When he came to an abrupt stop at the bottom, the stiff knee was bent double underneath him and he was sitting on his heel. Blood and joint fluids spilled into his knee; immediately it swelled to twice its size, and Dad moaned and cursed with the pain. Cal hurried to him and packed him down off the hill, jockeyed him into the back seat of our old blue '38 Ford, and drove him into Missoula to the doctor's office.

Dr. Turman said no bones were broken but that all the ligaments around the knee were torn. He thought Dad might eventually be able to get more motion out of the knee.

So after the initial swelling went down and the doctor gave them the go-ahead, every evening at bedtime Dad lay on his stomach on the bed while Mom sat at the foot of the bed and slowly, gently pressed his bum leg backward until he couldn't stand it anymore and gasped "Whoa!" She held it there while he grimaced and groaned and stood it as long as he could until he said, "Okay, let 'er back!" She slowly, carefully let up on the pressure. They repeated this six or eight times or as

My Big Tree became this lumber pile where Dad fell and injured his leg yet another time.

much as he could stand; he took a codeine pill and was done for that day. They were making a little progress toward increased motion.

Cal finished up the hand logging. He and Bill skidded the logs into a pile with horses, loaded them onto a truck with a crosshaul, and hauled them down to Fred Montelius's sawmill a couple of miles east of Clinton. Fred buzzed them into boards, and they hauled the lumber back and piled it back of the woodshed.

At the tail end of that winter Dad set a ladder against that twelve-foot lumber pile, crawled up on top, and began to add more boards to it. He was packing a plank across it when he slipped on a little skiff of snow and sat down hard with his bum knee under him again. This time he fractured the kneecap, and the doctor called a permanent halt to the nightly knee bends. The few inches of hard-won motion were lost. It was back on crutches until the fracture mended. Being on crutches did not mean he didn't work, for there was nothing wrong with his other leg or his two hands or his head; he merely used crutches to get from one place to another.

By June of '48 Dad hired a crew and began logging full-time for Western Lumber Mill (later Tree Farmers) up Starvation Gulch. On weekends that summer he dug the footings for his machine shed, and the next winter he and Grampa Mueller built it out of lumber that had once been my Big Tree.

I silently mourned the loss of my noble Big Tree. My getaway spot, my thinking place and refuge was reduced to a mere log, then boards. I climbed to the stump in the spring, but it just wasn't the same.

Thirty-five years later my own two girls' special spot was the Big Stump where they sat and surveyed their world. Their young eyes lovingly took in what I had seen a generation before: our narrow little Clark Fork River Valley with Swartz Creek across the way; Clinton, long and strung out off to their right; Dad's saddlehorse grazing in the three-cornered pasture; and the house, garage, and ranch buildings and the long machine shed nestled below. But they would never know, as I did, the sheltered feeling of the towering Big Tree above them.

THE SEARCH, 1951

THAT MORNING IN LATE APRIL the weather report said: "Rain today with probable snow in the mountains." Too wet for field work. So right after breakfast Dad left to ride the hills to check on the cattle, the condition of the feed, and the few cows that hadn't yet calved at turnout time.

Three years before, after he had logged off the state ground in the mountains behind his place, he went up in one of Johnson Flying Service's old Travelair planes and seeded the logged-off area from the air. The orchard grass had come in real good, and now he was eager to see how it looked this spring.

Dad had always told his family never to worry if he was late coming in from the hills. He assured them that if he couldn't get home before dark for some reason, he'd build a campfire, sleep out, and come on in when it got light enough to travel.

But by dusk that evening Rex and Mom were uneasy. Rex drove up to the corrals for a look around. There stood Dad's buckskin saddlehorse with his head down and the saddle under his belly.

"Jesus!"

Rex had a feeling that Dad was dead. He fought back panic. Knowing it was useless he called out once anyway on the slim chance that Dad was within hearing distance. A raven in the top of a dead fir mocked him, then only the silence of the woods. He pounded the pickup the mile back to the ranch headquarters and told Mom, "Buck's down at the corral with the saddle under his belly."

"Oh, my God," breathed Mom.

"I'm gonna go round up some men and go lookin' for 'im. He could be anywhere back there," Rex said.

First he left word at the Clinton Store, for it had the only phone around. Then he stopped briefly at three nearby ranches. Within minutes a dozen men converged on the corral where the buckskin still stood—some afoot, others on horseback, and all with rifles and flashlights or lanterns. After agreeing to fire one shot if they found him, the men spread out and searched and called into the rainy night.

Mom found herself alone, too shocky to cry, and with nothing to do but wait. She attacked the house, and as she furiously swept and dusted and pushed large furniture about long into the night, she thought of their life together.

She was the Clinton schoolmarm when she met Dad. He was a young man on crutches who had very recently been released from the hospital after a seven-month stay with a permanently injured right hip and leg. She was captivated by his big grin in a painfully thin face. She liked his enthusiasm, and he liked hers. They eloped. "Nineteen twenty-eight. Let's see, that would be twenty-three years ago now," she figured aloud.

She rearranged the kitchen cupboards using fresh newspapers as shelf paper, for thrift was part of her makeup. She thought of the times they had shared over those last twenty-three years, good things like their marriage, their son who worked the ranch with them, and their daughter now in nurses' training in Missoula. And there had been some pretty good cattle prices some years. The hard times came to her mind as well. The shop fire the winter of '37 that had forced them to start all over again. The loss of their baby boy in 1940. She couldn't think of her baby now, or she would not be able to function, and she *had* to function.

She rearranged the clothes closet, something she had been promising herself to do for some time, but there never seemed to be enough hours in a day to do all there was to do, what with three meals a day for her family and the various hired men, raising and preserving a garden big enough to be called a truck garden, tending the gas pumps, and making parts runs to town when the men were too busy. All of it bent toward their dream of a cattle ranch. At least it was Dad's dream, and Mom felt it was a wife's job to lend a hand in whatever presented itself. No one ever heard her express dissatisfaction with her lot, and so it was assumed that his dreams were her dreams. But she did get tired. That near-death from nephritis a few years ago had weakened her.

As she sorted clothes she wondered, "Is he dead? Is he alive but unconscious? Maybe he can't hear the men's calls. Did his bum leg somehow get hung up in the stirrup?" Enough! She decided the furniture could use a good polishing, something she'd never hoped to get to. She hunted up a dusty bottle of Old English Wax and a soft piece of old underwear.

The party of men fanned out over the hills behind Starvation Gulch, behind Connick Gulch, and into the saddle of the mountain where the salt lick was. They called. No answer. Startled cows and calves appeared in the lantern light, wide-eyed, questioning, surprised at this new apparition in the darkness. They quickly got to their feet and stood humped up watching the men as they climbed on.

Vern Baily, Don Roth, and Bob Montelius, following a set of shod horse tracks—which were fast becoming obliterated by the heavy rain—were the first to find Dad, lying below an old logging road. Vern's rifle shot brought the others to where Dad lay, the cold rain falling on him, his tiny fire nearly out, guarded by his shepherd-collie dog, Tip, who growled and threatened anyone coming near his Jim. No one could approach him until Dad reached out and got hold of Tip and said to him, "It's all right."

Then he spoke to the circle of men around him, "The son of a bitch threw me an' broke my hip again."

Men crowded around looking for ways to make him easier in any way they could. Others gathered up wood and got his tiny flickering fire to roaring in their enthusiastic relief that he'd been found alive. Someone headed back down to the Bonita Ranger Station for a stretcher while Rex, as good a hand as any grown man, went to get their flatbed truck, the only rig on the place low-geared enough to make it up the steep logging road to the landing. Calling out to Mom that Dad was alive but hurt, Rex threw an old mattress on the flatbed and growled it up the hill to the landing. Willing hands loaded Dad on the stretcher, carried him down the logging road to the landing, then placed him on the mattress. Tip jumped up on the flatbed beside his Jim, bared his teeth to all, and they took the wrenching ride off the hill and down to the house.

Meanwhile, Mom was so filled with relief that she stopped cleaning. "My house has never been cleaner, but what a price to pay for a clean house!" Now she could cry, but in the bedroom where no one could see her if they came in. And she calculated to have her tears cried out before they got back with Dad.

Someone had summoned an ambulance from Missoula. Dr. Turman, the old family doctor who had saved Dad's life and leg before, was already at the house when the neighbors bore the stretcher in and laid him on the davenport. On the ride downhill he had taken gulps of whiskey to kill the pain. It warmed him up some, and now it loosened his tongue.

"I was just startin' up a steep little pitch when the saddle slipped back with the cinch in Buck's flanks, an' he bucked me off. I went so high the crows started to build a nest in my ass. He kicked me while I was in the air an' broke the leg again. When I came down I landed right on my feet! *Je*-sus Chr-*ist*, it did hurt! Then the son of a bitch took off leavin' me there. I tried to get Tip to go home an' bring somebody back, but he wouldn't leave. This was around ten this mornin', an' it was damn cold an' rainin' like a dirty bastard. I scraped around an' got some sticks an' twigs, an' pine needles. I had a helluva time gettin' a fire goin' 'cause everything was so goddamn wet. I used my lighter to dry the pine needles off enough to finally get it goin'. I reached all around as far as I could reach with my hands for chips an' bark an' scraps. Then I got ahold of a little bitty limb an' I scraped around as far as that would reach an' got all there was. When they found me I'd run outa wood, an' was colder'n a welldigger's ass."

Dad arrived at the hospital at four in the morning on the 30th of April. At daylight he looked out his hospital window at four inches of fresh snow on the window ledge. Four inches at Missoula's elevation amounted to six or eight inches up in the hills, where only a few short hours ago he had lain immobile with the sixth serious injury to the same leg in the last twenty-six years.

DON'T ROCK THE ROUTINE

A LIGHT TAPPING on my door wakens me instantly. "Miss Flansburg." Another knock.

I sit straight up in bed.

Sister Mary Bede opens my door a crack and quietly says, "Miss Flansburg, your father is being brought into the emergency room. There's been an accident involving a horse. The night watchman is here to walk you over to the hospital."

I sit stunned.

"Miss Flansburg? Are you awake?"

"Yes, Sister." I galvanize into action and am out of bed reaching for my clothes. I dress in no time and walk down the darkened dormitory hall of St. Patrick School of Nursing. At this hour the lobby is lit only by the soft glow of the Virgin Mary who stands with her perpetual benign expression, palms outstretched, calmly stepping on an evil-looking open-mouthed snake. That snake has always looked altogether too real for my taste, and now in the half-light of four in the morning it gives me the creeps.

The night watchman holds the doors open for me, and we step out into the late April night. A good inch of new snow covers the sidewalk of Pine Street.

"Yep, it started coming down a couple hours ago," he says.

We walk the block to the north door of the old Main, the original St. Patrick Hospital where Dad had spent seven months recovering from the 1925 logging accident.

"What happened, d'you know?" I ask.

He doesn't. Only that "they're bringing him in an ambulance from Clinton, and it has something to do with a horse."

That seems strange to me because Dad was raised horseback. Then I remember he had had another horse accident when I was four. Five or six of his horses had got out onto the highway. Dad saddled up Nig, his cutting horse, to run them back in. Down the highway they all came as tight as they could go, past the barn, out in front of the gas pumps.

As Dad told it later, "Nig was shod. I had it figured I'd be off the oil in a couple more jumps an' then I'd turn 'em."

But his calculations didn't include the unexpected. Mom ran out and flapped her apron at the bunch trying to help head them off. They thundered past her, but Nig, right on their heels, spooked and turned on a dime. His iron shoes slipped on the pavement; he fell and skidded twenty feet down the highway with Dad's bum leg underneath him. The force of it ground all the metal hooks off Dad's boot.

The still shots of my memory are of traffic stopped both ways, people milling around, a man holding Nig's reins, the bunch of loose horses across the road over on the railroad right-of-way with their heads up, nostrils flaring, stepping high and tasting freedom, and Dad sitting in the middle of the highway grimacing and untwisting the right pant leg of his Levi's that was wound around his leg like a barber pole. As I watched from the window, several men loaded him up into the back seat of a car and drove off.

My next memory is of Mom and me visiting him here in St. Pat's Hospital in the big ward. He was lying comfortably, his hands clasped behind his head, grinning at us.

"Hi, Daddy!"

"How's my good girl?"

"Fine . . . See?" I held up the treat Mama had bought me, a brand-new kind of gum called Dentyne. It came in a little block and was scored so you could break it off one little piece at a time.

Mom prompted, "Would you like to share your gum with your dad?"

I rather reluctantly handed him the hunk of gum, and he looked it over, took a big chaw off it, and handed it back. I took it, looked at the teeth marks on the third that was left, and said not a word. I decided he just hadn't seen any gum like that before and didn't know he was supposed to break off one piece. Besides, he had a broken leg so I would forgive him.

The next day he came home in a cast. For a few days he didn't go out to work, so I got to lean on his bed and visit or play Old Maid with him.

The night watchman and I mount the hospital steps. Dread of what I might find rises up in my throat, but I swallow it down and walk the fast walk of a student nurse down the cavernous, high-ceilinged hall to the stairs and up to the third floor. Familiar odors of old Third Main reach me—the ether of the operating room and the sour smell of the hopper room between the two big wards—and at the top of the stairs I hear Dad's voice. He's conscious! I enter the tiny room they call the emergency room.

Dad is lying on a stretcher looking like he has looked for years. He has a full head of gray and white hair, a good faceful of quarter-inch salt-and-pepper whiskers, and sharp blue eyes that see everything from under bushy gray eyebrows. He is shivering and talking loudly telling those around him what happened.

"I warmed rocks in the fire an' held 'em up agin my ass t'keep from freezin' t'death," he tells me. I giggle partly because he is still tiddly from the whiskey he drank for the pain while they were getting him down off the hill, and partly because I am so relieved he is alive and feisty. I feel proud of what a remarkable and resourceful fellow my dad is.

The X-ray shows the ball of the right hip is fractured, which happened when his saddlehorse kicked him in midair. Surprisingly, it also shows that when Dad came down to earth and lit on his feet, the ball was driven up into the socket and "set."

Our Dr. Turman is here. He is intimately acquainted with that particular leg and knows that any unnecessary fooling around with it will further compromise its already poor circulation. He will not operate; it is already set well enough. He orders that Dad be given a hypo and put to bed.

Dad is wheeled to 304, a private room in the new end of the hospital called the Annex. I fuss around with pillows and extra blankets to get him comfortable, then plant myself in a chair to stay with him the rest of the night. The doctor gently tells me that Dad is all right and that it won't be necessary for me to stay. He says he will cast it in the morning, and if all goes well he will probably go home the next day; but the first order of business is to get him warmed up, pain-free, and rested after his nearly eighteen hours of exposure.

It's hard for me to leave. He's my dad. But I tell him to get some rest and I'll be back before I go on duty in the morning.

I amble back down the Annex hall and up the ramp to where the chart room perches between Annex and Main. I want to tell the night nurse to let me know if Dad gets worse, but the chart room's empty. Then I realize it's 5:30 in the morning and that both student night nurses (one on Annex and one on Main) are out on the floor giving what is charted as "early AM care." This rigidly enforced hospital routine consists of waking all the patients with a pan of wash water, not

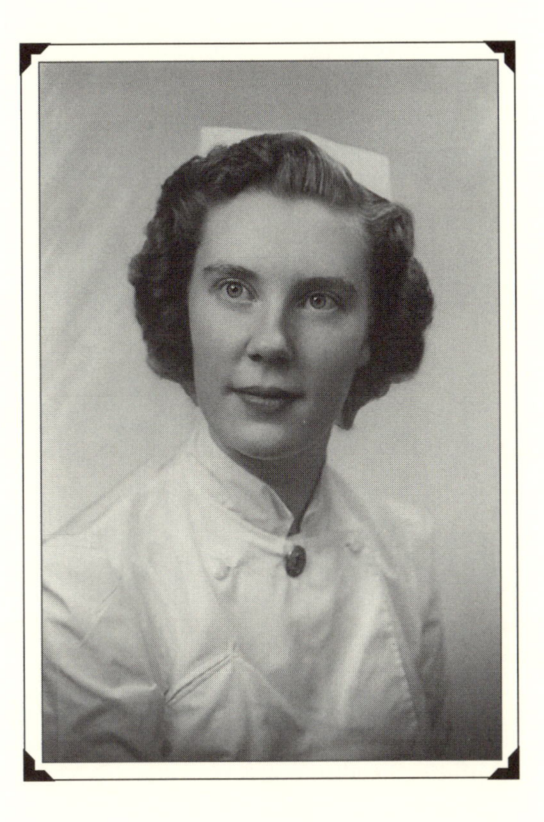

My class picture, St. Patrick School of Nursing in Missoula, class of '51.

merely a damp washcloth, and washing their hands and faces for breakfast, offering the bedpan and/or urinal, emptying and recording same, getting fresh drinking water, and straightening their beds. For each night nurse to get through this job for fifteen to twenty-six patients apiece, she has to start out on this errand of mercy by 4:00 A.M. From that hour on, both student nurses sprint along at top speed with all the corner-cutting efficiency and time management they can muster. Then it's hypos or pain pills for nearly everyone, for now that they have been roused at that ungodly hour they hurt. Or they're mad. Or both.

I decide nobody'd have time to call me if he does get worse, so I slowly head for the stairs on Main. Call lights are on all over. Main's night nurse passes me racing for the far end of her hall bearing a pan of wash water in one hand, a pitcher of ice water in the other, and an emptied urinal in its bag dangling from a little finger. I am glad my night rotations are behind me. Tired now from the letdown of relief, I slowly go down the dark stairs, down the hall, and out the north door. I notice it has snowed some more, at least two inches since I came through here an hour and a half ago.

After the day shift begins my supervisor gives me permission to go see Dad a minute. It seems there has already been a discussion at morning report and a consensus of opinion concerning the doctor's scandalous orders for 304. Considering the history of that blood-poor leg it is logical to move Dad as little as possible; therefore, the doctor's orders are for a hypo at 7:45 followed at 8:00 by a cast application in his room.

The nun in charge of the floor collars me. She is outraged. She lets me know in no uncertain terms that casting in a patient's room is *not done*; it will only make a *big mess* in his room; there is a special cast room on Main for that purpose; all the *other* doctors use it; and hospital policy is to be adhered to! I try to get a word in to explain the reason, but I am too rattled by her loud tirade. I end up just standing there in the hall enduring her wrath. This sharp-tongued Sister has always been able to cow me down. I am puzzled about what I am supposed to be doing about all this; it's the doctor she should be talking to. Maybe she has, and just when she was hunting her hole to get away from the doctor's wrath I came along. Who knows?

A little farther on down the hall the head nurse motions me into the Annex hopper room and conspiratorily urges me to use my influence to get another doctor for Dad.

"Why?"

She informs me that the X-ray shows the ball of the joint is rammed up into the socket; it needs surgery to repair it; the doctor *isn't even going to operate* to set it properly; and he's not even letting them load my father onto a stretcher to wheel him to the cast room. She delivers her appeal in a buddy-buddy, one-nurse-to-another sort of way so that I will convince Dad to let one of the bone men take over the case.

Now her I can talk to, and I tell her the history of that leg and our doctor's intimate knowledge of it. She is kindly but unconvinced. I am likewise unconvinced by her opinion and I'm maddened by the hospital's official point of view. I'll say nothing to Dad of this discussion until he goes home. No use to get him on the fight.

"Morning, Dad."

"Hello there! Take a look at that." He bobs his head toward the window where four inches of new snow sits on the sill. "There's prob'ly a good six inches up in the hills behind Starvation. Wouldn't that be a helluva note to be lyin' up there in that right now?"

I leave and the doctor puts on the cast in the room assisted by the head nurse and the orderly.

The orderly stops me in the hall later and gets in his two bits' worth. Officious and talking loudly, he informs me of the mess that was made in the room; the cast room was supposed to be where you applied casts; it was the loosest cast he had ever seen put on and couldn't possibly be of any use; and it's too bad I couldn't have talked my dad into getting a good doctor.

The French nun strikes out with venom: "Well, I guess we have to put up with these old docteur!"

Thus the official pronouncement has been made. Everyone from the head nun down to the orderly adheres to the party line—The Rules, Hospital Policy, The Way We've Always Done It. It all comes under the same heading as having to waken sick patients at four in the morning to wash for breakfast. I am plumb fed up with this whole layout. Only four months to graduation.

At 3:00 P.M. I get off duty and drop in to see Dad a minute.

"How are ya, Dad?"

"Finer'n frog hair," he answers. "Doc says I c'n go home in the mornin'. The cast'll be good'n dry by then."

I drag back to my room at the School of Nursing. Fatigue dogs my tracks, for it's been a long, emotional day. I'm mad yet at the whole Third Floor. I pass through the lobby. The Virgin Mary is still standing there with her foot on the serpent. That damn snake is still alive and well. I saw him in action today.

THE LEG

AFTER THAT INJURY, Dad wore a body cast from his right knee to his rib cage for four months. After a couple of weeks home in bed, he was out working.

That summer he hayed for Lewis Richards, who leased the Doc Turman place next to our place at Clinton. Haying was mechanized by then. Richards mowed, raked, and stacked while Dad ran the Farmhand. Wearing his half body cast he bounced over the fields and little ditch banks scooping up hay and setting it up on the haystack. By the end of August when he took the cast off, the cast was "all broke to hell and rattled like a sack of marbles." But it had served its purpose, for the hip had healed.

His bum foot froze every winter. Pus bulged against the big scab on the side of his heel. He rubbed the foot and gritted his teeth while he worked one end of the scab loose to release the pressure. Either he or Mom bandaged it, and he went on about his day's work on his logging job or on the ranch or in the shop. Only his eyes sunken under bushy gray eyebrows let on he was hurting.

Each successive injury had compromised the circulation even more. The sores on both sides of the foot took longer and longer to heal until the foot itself had become a source of infection. Twenty-nine years after his initial injury, Dad and his doctor decided it was finally time to cut the leg off. On March 8th, 1954, Dr. Turman amputated the leg halfway between the knee and the ankle.

A woman who worked in the hospital's kitchen told me that the old foot and leg were wrapped in paper and taken to the kitchen freezer until someone could run it over to the pathologist's office. It tickled Dad to learn that some wag had labeled it "leg of lamb."

The day after his amputation he got on crutches and raced me, his eight-months-pregnant daughter, down the hospital hall and he won hands down. A week later he was plowing the fields on the Starvation Creek place.

Mom and Dad in 1954; Dad now has a wooden leg.

As soon as Dad's stump healed sufficiently he drove himself to Schindler's in Spokane and came back with a new wooden leg. The old boot and brace were retired; now he sported two legs and two feet, both shod in brand-new White loggers.

Like his father before him, Dad wore black wool long underwear year-round. Now he cut the right leg of his underwear off at the knee to accommodate the wooden leg. One morning when he was dressing we all heard a sudden "God damn, dirty rotten, son of a bitch!" He had cut the wrong leg off a brand-new pair of underwear.

The next year Dad bought an old jayhawk stacker for its angle iron at an auction sale in the Cold Springs area on the low bald hills south of Missoula. The following day he and Rex drove to the auction site in two rigs: a pickup truck carrying a cutting torch, and a ton-and-a-half truck to haul the angle iron. Rex unloaded the cutting torch and took off for town on errands. Dad began to cut off the iron.

He finished up with the cutting torch, then stepped inside the stacker arms and began to crawl around on the ground twisting off bolts with a wrench. The foot of the wooden leg accidently tripped the dog that held the stacker up off the ground. The stacker fell four feet onto his prosthetic leg and snapped his real leg bone off just below his knee.

"There was nobody around, an' it had me pinned, so while I waited for Rex to get back I kept takin' off bolts as far around as I could reach," he told us later.

Gus Wornath and Henry Rehder happened by to pick up their auction purchases, and they released him from his trap just as Rex drove up.

Rex said, "We'll get you loaded up in the pickup and take you right to the hospital, Dad."

"No, by God! We're gonna load up this iron *first*!"

Whatever Dad said was the way you did it, so while Rex loaded up the iron, Dad took off his wooden leg. Then he refused to ride in the pickup. Just like Grampa who'd insisted on riding Old Riley down off the hill with a broken pelvis, Dad insisted he be helped into the driver's seat of the truck. And with his broken leg hanging over the edge of the seat, he drove himself up to the door of the hospital. Dr. Turman cast it, and he was home the next day.

"D'you have a hole in your leg like that?"

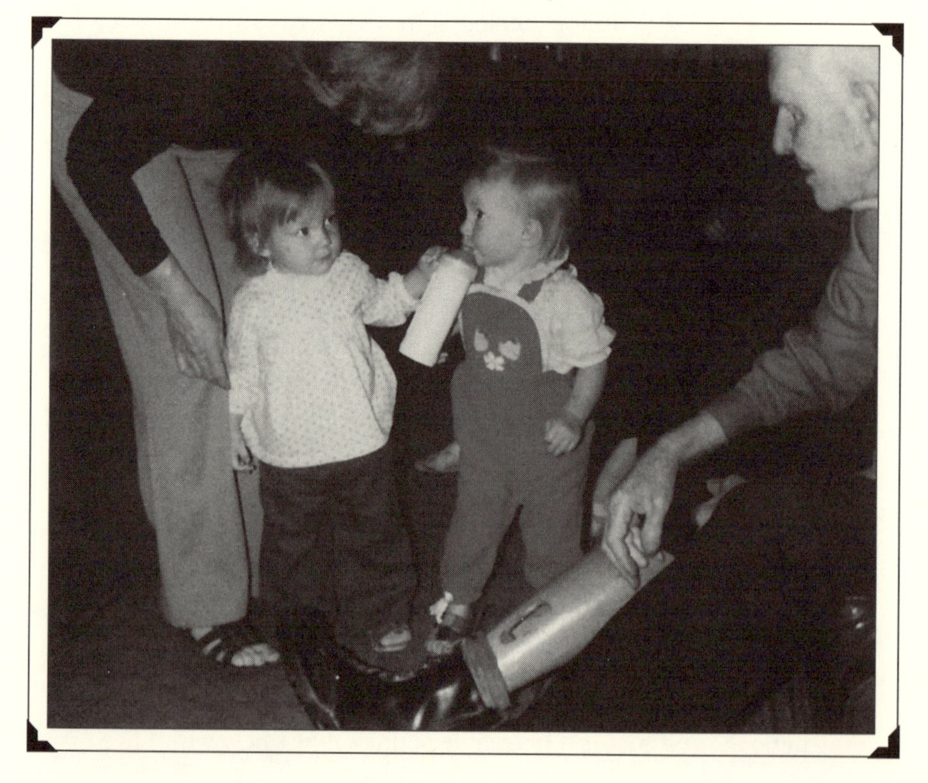

The next week he was plowing fields on the Starvation Creek place.

It is 1984, and my two daughters, Ruth and Laura, have two-year-old daughters of their own.

Dad pulls up his right pant leg revealing his artificial leg to his two little great-granddaughters. "D'you have a hole in your leg like that?" he asks them.

Their eyes widen as they stare at the hole in the side of Grampa Jim's strange-looking leg. He sticks his fingers in the hole. Sarah gives her mother a questioning look: "Is this a safe situation or not?" Trisha ventures closer, curious but not at all sure of this oddity. She puts out one pudgy forefinger and tentatively touches the leg. Dad knocks his knuckles on the hollow leg, and both little girls pull back and open their big eyes even wider. They're speechless. It's the strangest-looking thing they've ever seen.

Dad is delighted with the little girls' reactions. For the last sixty years he has been having "fun," first with his real leg, then with the wooden one.

THE HILLS OF HOME

ON THIS WARM AUGUST MORNING of my sixty-third birthday I sit here on Rex's front porch looking up the narrow gulch and at the steep mountains that rise up on either side of it. I feel embraced by these hills where my roots have grown deep. I gaze with fond familiarity at ponderosa pines sprinkled over their hot, dry south faces and at the cool, moist north slopes where fir trees grow as thick as hair on a dog's back.

Gramma and Grampa Flansburg and their nine kids lived here the years between 1916 and 1924 in an old three-room frame house and a bunkhouse that sat out of sight farther up the gulch. Nothing remains of those buildings except a square-headed nail here and there. The family earned their living horse-logging these draws and ridges.

Dad loads logs on a wagon with his canthook on a cross haul. This was taken at what is now called West Riverside, near Milltown, Montana.

I idly watch a raven flap over to Clinton a quarter mile away. His unswerving flight takes him across a field, a frontage road, Montana Rail Links railroad tracks, and the Old Mullan Road to a faded building that was once a livery stable called Dunnigan's Barn. In 1907 Dan Dunnigan bought that land from a mining company and built this first building on it. In 1925 Dunnigan's Barn became Johnny Baird's bright orange Clinton Garage and Grocery Store. In 1927 Dad bought it, and the next year in that old building he and Mom began their fifty-six years together. In 1935 Dad sold the Old Place, as we called it, to George and Olive Dawley, whose three little girls were my first preschool playmates and are still my close friends these many years later. Eventually Don and Lucille Norton bought it and have lived there nearly fifty years. That Old Place has been lived in continuously for at least eighty-five years and hasn't been painted since 1925 when Baird painted it orange. Don Norton says, "Hell, I ain't gonna paint it. The county'd just want more taxes!"

Though I married and went my way, Rex stayed with our parents all their lives, worked alongside of them, and faithfully cared for them until they died. The summer of 1989, while rewiring the shop, Rex fell

My brother, Rex.

Rex's place in the mouth of Connick Gulch.

through the shop ceiling thirteen feet to the cement floor, landing on the base of his spine. Miraculously he was neither killed nor paralyzed. His shattered third lumbar vertebra was surgically repaired with metal plates and screws. Although he recovered, the heavy work he had done all his life was no longer possible. He sold the ranch but reserved Connick Gulch; and seventy-five years after our Dad's family first moved here, Rex built his home here within sight of the Old Place. The circle is complete.

I love these hills of home. That brushy sidehill to my right is where I lost my brand-new winter jacket, forest green with orange and yellow embroidery on the front. I was thirteen then. I had tied it to the back of my saddle in granny knots that worked loose. When I discovered it was gone, Dad and I rode back and forth over the hillside where we had been, but no luck. Dad said not a word about it, but acted as if it was just one of those unfortunate things that happens now and then. I was surprised and relieved, for I'd expected a chewing out.

That jacket zipper is still up there, I suppose. Probably trampled deep into some game trail over these last fifty years. . . .

EPILOGUE

I WAS SEVEN YEARS OLD. Gramma Mueller and I were walking down Higgins Avenue in Missoula. Right in front of Peterson's Drug Store, where my parents bought all our prescriptions, I suddenly thought about my daddy. I began to limp and rack over exactly like he did.

Gramma was embarrassed. "Walk right," she said.

I paid no attention but continued to hobble along just like Daddy.

"People are staring," she hissed, but I didn't notice for I was having fun being like my daddy. Gramma was mortified. She picked at my sleeve. "Stop that!"

But only when I was ready, when it ceased to be fun, did I "walk right."

When I grew up I became "just like daddy" in other ways. I inherited his love of ragtime and a good time, and his ability to work efficiently. On the flip side I, too, became a driver of myself and everybody else and fell heir to his plague of periodic dark depressions.

Dad faced the world like the rim of a wheel protecting his family from harm and wrestling out a living for us. Mom was the hub of that wheel. We all rotated around her as she listened to us, worked with us, and helped us talk out problems to find solutions. With a few words she showed us a truth or another viewpoint to ponder. She talked Dad up from his discouragements and down from his rages.

We kids worshiped Dad, but we were not on his level because talking to him was like talking to God. Mom interpreted Dad and us kids to each other; had it not been so, Dad and Rex and I would never have known or appreciated each other like we did. His all-knowing, all-powerful aura and our fear and worship of him stood in the way. Mom was our common denominator who held us all together.

Dad was such a strong figure in my upbringing that I grew up believing it was necessary to have a man to take care of me, that I couldn't do it on my own. I also believed a woman's place was in the home unless she *had* to make the living.

Dad. This picture was taken by Mary Purington for a profile she wrote, published in the Montana Journal, *March-April 1991.*

What I really wanted was a home, husband, and children, and to stay home and take care of them like my mother did. For some of us young women fresh out of nurses' training the goals were: (1) to marry well (whatever that meant) and (2) to work at nursing only if we had to. Mom always said, "You must have a profession to fall back on." Many times since, I've been glad for that ability to get work.

A year out of nurses' training I married George Hedgers, a man seventeen years my senior, a man I did not love (although I swore to myself and everybody else that I did) because I thought he could take care of me.

"I'll give ya five years," Dad said.

I had inherited his stubbornness, too, and stuck it out nearly twenty years, way longer than I should have, trying to make the best of a bad bargain. My two children, Ruth and Laura, were born of this marriage.

Three and a half years later I married Dick Haaglund and became stepmother to Laurel, Mike, Dave, and Lanel. Sadly this marriage ended, too, after fourteen years. Now I enjoy living alone in home country between Clinton and Missoula. I keep in touch with Rex and my six children and seventeen grandchildren, and life is good.

Over the years Dad and Mom gathered up bottomland and hill land (Starvation Gulch, the mouth of Wallace Gulch, and Connick Gulch) and farmed and raised cattle. In 1969 when the freeway took out their home, shop, and ranch buildings, they moved again to Wallace Gulch across from the Clinton interchange. To get out of debt Dad logged at Lincoln, Montana, for seven years while Rex kept the ranch going.

In 1984 Mom died of a sudden heart attack at eighty years old. Three and a half years later and five weeks short of his eighty-fourth birthday Dad died in his sleep in a Missoula nursing home where he had lived the last year of his life. Our parents left us the fruits of their industry—a trust fund to me and the ranch to Rex.

Life handed Mom and Dad a daunting set of circumstances and a tough time to live in, yet they prevailed. They were living examples of hard work, know-how, thrift, and how to get by and even get ahead in spite of hard times. One usually does not forget what is learned at a parent's or a grandparent's knee.

Tough times take on many forms, and each generation walks through its own fires. Eunice and Jim Flansburg's children and grandchildren feel equipped to prevail over whatever fires they will be called upon to walk through. And that is riches.